SHAMELESS

SHAME-LESS

A SEXUAL REFORMATION

NADIA BOLZ-WEBER

CONVERGENT
NEW YORK

CONVERGENT BOOKS is a registered trademark and its C colophon
is a trademark of Penguin Random House LLC.

Library of Congress Cataloging-in-Publication Data
Names: Bolz-Weber, Nadia, author.
Title: Shameless : a sexual reformation / Nadia Bolz-Weber.
Description: [New York] : Convergent, [2019]
Identifiers: LCCN 2018021697 (print) | LCCN 2018045560 (ebook) |
ISBN 9781601427601 (e-book) | ISBN 9781601427588 (hardcover)
Subjects: LCSH: Sex—Religious aspects—Christianity. | Sex—Biblical teaching.
Classification: LCC BT708 (ebook) | LCC BT708 .B65 2019 (print) |
DDC 261.8/357—dc23
LC record available at https://lccn.loc.gov/2018021697

ISBN 978-1-60142-758-8
Ebook ISBN 978-1-60142-760-1

Printed in the United States of America

Book design by Patrice Sheridan
Chapter opener illustrations by Prrrint!
Jacket design by Sarah Horgan
Jacket and title page illustration: "Eve" by John Martin/© British Library Board.
All Rights Reserved. Bridgeman Images

1 3 5 7 9 10 8 6 4 2

First Edition

FOR E.B.

CONTENTS

NOTE TO READERS

———

The stories in this book that come from my own life are true to my memory. As with any recollection of the past, how I remember and tell the story, along with how my parishioners remember and tell their stories, may differ from how others may have recalled the same events. In some cases, identifying details have been changed to protect the identity of others. In places I have condensed time to aid narrative flow. The stories from my parishioners are all told with their permission.

I also wish to let you know that stories of sexual abuse and assault came up with disturbing regularity in my interviews. I am not equipped to address this particular harm within the scope of this book. But neither could I fail to mention it.

At the end of this book is a short list of books, curricula, and educators that can help you talk about your own story, and listen to the stories of others. I was terrified when we started conversations about sex and spirituality at church. But it was amazing. Do it.

NOTE TO READERS

The stories in this book that come from my own life are true to my memory. As with any recollection of the past, how I remember and tell the story, along with how my parishioners remember and tell their stories, may differ from how others may have recalled the same events. In some cases, identifying details have been changed to protect the identity of others. In places I have condensed time to aid narrative flow. The stories from my parishioners are all told with their permission.

I also wish to let you know that stories of sexual abuse and assault came up with disturbing regularity in my interviews. I am not equipped to address this particular harm within the scope of this book. But neither could I fail to mention it.

At the end of this book is a short list of books, curricula, and educators that can help you talk about your own story, and listen to the stories of others. I was terrified when we started conversations about sex and spirituality at church. But it was amazing. Do it.

SHAMELESS

SHAMELESS

INVOCATION

The week Prince died, I was flying to Charlotte, North Carolina, to speak to a group of Methodists. That same week, the state legislature of North Carolina voted in the so-called bathroom bill, which stated that people must use the bathroom that corresponds to the gender on their driver's license. As I stuffed my carry-on bag beneath the seat in front of me, I thought of this hideous bill and the little plan I had concocted to protest it. My bag contained a roll of Scotch tape and half a dozen sheets of paper, all which bore—in huge purple print—the androgynous symbol for Prince's name.

The plane took off, and I looked out the window. We were traveling over the dry plains of eastern Colorado, thirty thousand feet above a dot matrix of green and brown circles that revealed the geometry of industrial agriculture. As a city girl who doesn't know a thing about farming, I've always found those green circles puzzling. Why would farmers plant circles of crops in lots that are square?

When I looked into it later, I discovered that in 1940, just twenty-nine miles from the spot where my plane made its way into the crisp Colorado sky, a man named Frank Zybach invented the center-pivot irrigation system, essentially revolutionizing farming in America. In his system, the watering equipment turns on a pivot, allowing sprinklers to water crops in a circular pattern. The crops aren't planted in circles; they're just watered that way. The water never gets to the crops in the corners.

When I arrived at the Charlotte airport, I went about my project of taping the purple Prince symbols over bathroom signs that read "Men" and "Women." Then I went to church.

The day after I returned home, I sat on the edge of the stage at House for All Sinners and Saints (HFASS), the Denver church I pastor. My parishioner Meghan and I were watching the church's monthly community meal take place. Groups of mismatched people of differing ages and sexual and gender orientations were situated at twelve circular tables throughout the room, eating chili out of Styrofoam bowls.

Meghan, a large transwoman with long, thin hair and a face and figure that she admits do not allow her to "pass," has enough social anxiety to make sitting at a communal table a non-starter, so she usually makes her own place on the edge of the stage. Some Sundays, rather than join the fray, I hang with her and talk comic books.

That day, as our legs hung off the stage, I brought up something that had been on my mind lately. "Hey, Meghan, I read my old Christian sex-ed book this morning for the first time in maybe forty years." She laughed, and I went on. "It taught me that God's plan is for everyone to be a hetero-sexual, cis-gender Christian who never has sex with anyone until they marry their one true love and make babies."*

We both laughed. Then I shook my head. "I mean, I do think there are genuinely those kinds of people out there. . . ."

Meghan held up her hand and touched her thumb to the rest of her purple nail-polished fingers. "Sure there are. And this is how small that circle is."

If you were to draw a circle that represents all the people on the planet, and then inside it draw another small circle to represent the people who live according to "God's plan," then, well, very few people on the planet fit in *that* circle. Meghan doesn't fit in that circle. I don't fit in that circle. Also not included in the circle are divorced people, people in unhappy marriages, people who have sex before mar-riage, people who masturbate, asexuals, gay people, bisexu-als, people who are not Christian, people who are gender non-binary . . .

If that's "God's plan," then God planned poorly.

---

* The term "cis-gender" means that the biological sex assigned to some-one at birth matches their gender identity.

Maybe you don't fit into that circle, either. God planted so many of us in the corners, yet the center-pivot irrigation of the church's teachings about sex and sexuality tends to exclude us. Many of us were taught that if you do not fit inside the circle of the church's behavioral codes, God is not pleased with you, so we whittled ourselves down to a shape that could fit those teachings, or we denied those parts of ourselves entirely. The lusty parts. The kinky parts. The gay parts. The unwanted-pregnancy parts. The unfulfilled parts.

But our sexual and gender expressions are as integral to who we are as our religious upbringings are. To separate these aspects of ourselves—to separate life as a sexual being from a life with God—is to bifurcate our psyche, like a musical progression that never comes to resolution.

In the ten years I've been pastor at HFASS, I've known young married couples who did what the church told them and "waited," only to discover that they could not, on the day of their wedding, flip a switch in their brains and in their bodies and suddenly go from relating to sex as sinful and dirty and dangerous to relating to sex as joyful and natural and God-given. I've known single women who didn't have sex until they were forty and now have absolutely no idea how to manage the emotional aspect of a sexual relationship. I've heard middle-aged women admit that they still can't make themselves wear a V-neck because as teenagers they were told female modesty was the best protection from unwanted male sexual advances. I've seen gay men who never reported the sexual abuse they experienced in the church because the church told them being gay was a sin. I've heard stories from women who experienced marital rape after getting married at twenty years old (because if you have to wait until marriage to have sex, then you hurry that shit up) but got the message from their church that because there is a verse in the Bible that says women should be subject to their husbands, it was not actually rape.

It doesn't feel very difficult to draw a direct line between the messages many of us received from the church and the harm we've experienced in our bodies and spirits as a result. So my argument in this book is this: we should not be more loyal to an idea, a doctrine, or an interpretation of a Bible verse than we are to *people*. If the teachings of the church are harming the bodies and spirits of people, we should rethink those teachings.

Five hundred years ago, Martin Luther took a hard look at the harm in his own parishioners' spiritual lives, specifically their torment from trying to fulfill the sacramental obligations that the church determined would appease an angry God. Seeing this, Luther dared to think that the Gospel—the story of God coming to humanity in Jesus of Nazareth, and speaking to us the words of life—could free his parishioners from the harm their own church had done them. Luther was less loyal to the teachings of the church than he was to *people*, and this helped spark what is now known as the Protestant Reformation.

I know that there will be those who do not wish to rethink their ideas about sexual ethics, gender, orientation, extramarital sex, and the inherent goodness of the human body. Maybe some people reading this will look at their own lives and in their own churches and see only happy, straight couples who have fulfilling monogamous sex and who glow with the satisfaction of "living in God's special plan for humanity." I don't know. Maybe. I don't go to your church and I do not live your life. So if the traditional teachings of the church around sex and the body have caused no harm in the lives of the people around you, and have even provided them a plan for true human flourishing, then this book probably is not for you. (Good news, though: the Christian publishing world is your oyster. There you'll find no lack of books to uphold and even help you double down on your beliefs.)

This book is for everyone else. It is water, I hope, for those planted in the corners. It is for anyone who has had to keep their love life secret. It is for all those who have been good and done everything right in the eyes of the church, and yet still have a sex life minus the fireworks and magic that were promised them if they just "waited." It is for the parents of the gay son, parents who love and support him because they know he is neither a mistake nor an aberrant sinner, and as a result of that support have become outsiders in their own church. This book is for everyone who ever felt ashamed of their sexual nature because of what someone told them in God's name. This book is for anyone who has walked away from Christianity and yet still is secretly into Jesus and always will be. This book is for anyone who has passed the traditional teachings of the church on sex to their own kids and now regrets it. This book is for the newly divorced man or woman who desires to be a caring and thoughtful lover, yet wonders: *Do the rules I learned in youth group still apply to me now?* This book is for the young Evangelical who silently disagrees with their church's stance on sex and sexual orientation, yet feels alone in that silence.

This book is for anyone who wonders, even subconsciously: *Has the church obsessed over this too much? Do we really think we've gotten it right?*

I believe strongly that the church, in general, has absolutely *not* gotten it right.

But to be fair, religion is not the only source of harmful messages about sex and the body. In American culture, as in the church, sex is a big deal. The broader culture bombards us with its commodification of sex, its own demeaning ideas about our value and currency. It draws its own small circle around, for instance, those human bodies that are deserving of desire—those with a particular symmetry of face, length of leg, ratio of fat to muscle, shape of eye, smoothness of skin—and those that are not deserving. We constantly assess how close we are to that ideal, or how far. We become invisible when we grow too old, too fat, too average to fit inside the small circle of desirability. This, along with the pervasive lie of *not enough*—not having enough sex, not having a partner who is sexy enough, not having a life that is exciting enough—can dull our ability to appreciate the pleasure of our actual bodies, our actual relationships, and our actual lives.

But I will not indulge in the sin of false equivalency. To admit that both the church and our culture can cause harm is not the same as saying the harm from both is equivalent. It is not. Because as harmful as the messages from society are, what society does not do is say that these messages are from *God*. Our culture does not say to me that the creator of the universe is disgusted by my cellulite.

So where do we go from here?

Well, I'd like for us, together, to reconsider what we've been told and what we've internalized from the church. Let us consider the harm that has been caused in God's name, but let's not be satisfied with stopping there. We must reach for a new Christian sexual ethic.

For nearly two years I have interviewed many of my parishioners, who have become the main characters of this book.* I have also shared stories from my own life, collected and read Christian sex-ed books, dived down a few rabbit holes (the temperance movement, the legacy of the church fathers, the little-known backstory of how Evangelicals took up the cause of abortion), studied Bible passages and Christian theology, and exhausted my friends by engaging a single topic of conversation for longer than any sane person ever should. I haven't so much written this book as I have been possessed by it.

As you read, please know that what I have given you are my best and most agonized-over ideas for recalibrating how we think about sex. And in all of it, I hope to aid the process of healing in those of us who have been hurt by the church's broader teachings or hurt by our own inability to even talk about sex at all. As individuals and communities, we continue to stutter when the subject comes up, to get sucker-punched by messages of judgment and shame, to get it wrong.

---

* The interviews that served as the case study for this book were exclusively with the people of House for All Sinners and Saints. As such, the stories are not representative of anything but what was shared with me by the people in a single congregation. My hope is that more communities, ones that represent a wider range of experiences and social locations, have similar conversations and share what they find.

You should know ahead of time that there's no chance I'm going to be able to address every sexual experience or variation or perspective in this book. I'm also not going to be able to address or even anticipate every objection to what I've written. I am not a sex therapist, or a historian, or a Bible scholar, or a cultural critic. What I am is a pastor who is concerned for the harm I see in my parishioners' lives and who is also concerned for you. I don't have answers, exactly. I have no updated list of good behaviors and bad behaviors. This book does not attempt to redeem the handful of Bible verses that have been weaponized against us. It is not a systematic theology of sex.

Here's what this book *is*. It is a DNA test of our own harm, pricking our arms, drawing the blood, and showing us where we came from so that we know how to step toward something new. It offers layers of stories and voices and perspectives and history and poetry and scripture. Like a human body, it has curves.

Alain de Botton, a philosopher, atheist, and bestselling author, argues that at least religion seems to understand the importance and power of sex.* Perhaps so. Sex is such a foundational part of us. When it is manipulated or exploited or denied, it can affect us in devastating ways. This is why religion has so often attempted to mitigate sex's power,

---

* "Only religions still take sex seriously. . . . Religions are often mocked for being prudish, but they wouldn't judge sex to be quite so bad if they didn't also understand that it could be rather wonderful." Alain de Botton, "Twelve Rude Revelations About Sex," *Psychology Today*, January 2, 2013.

whether through forced celibacy, modest dress, chastity belts, genital mutilation, pernicious lies taught to children about the dangers of masturbation, or any number of other things. But what I wonder is this: If religion has been the venue in which the power of sex is taken most seriously, could it also become the place in which a new conversation about it arises? One that is not afflicted with legalism and shaming, and yet also does not ignore the depravity of human beings in favor of some delusional idea that we are capable of perfect selflessness?

Can we who have been raised within a broadly Christian culture, if not squarely within the church, be a people who strive for the sexual flourishing of all people? And if so, where can we look for guidance?

For one, we could consider the World Health Organization's definition of sexual health:

A state of physical, emotional, mental and social well-being in relation to sexuality; not merely the absence of disease, dysfunction or infirmity. Sexual health requires a positive and respectful approach to sexuality and sexual relationships, as well as the possibility of having pleasurable and safe sexual experiences, free of coercion, discrimination and violence. For sexual health to be attained and maintained, the sexual rights of all persons must be respected, protected and fulfilled.*

---

* World Health Organization, "Defining Sexual Health," 2006, http://www.who.int/reproductivehealth/topics/sexual_health/sh_definitions/en.

In other words, consent (enthusiastic consent—not merely the absence of "no") and mutuality (enjoyment by both parties) are what the WHO says constitute a baseline sexual ethic.

Yet, as critical as consent and mutuality are, a Christian sexual ethic must offer more than this. And as counterintuitive as it might seem, the place I'm suggesting we look to for help is the Bible. The Bible is simply too potent to be left to those who would use it, even unwittingly, to justify and protect their own place in the center of the irrigation field. And sometimes the origin of the harm can be the most powerful source of its healing.

I'm stealing another move from Martin Luther here. In Luther's *Small Catechism*, he teaches that the Ten Commandments are about more than the mere absence of bad behavior. They're also about the presence of good. For instance, you would think that fulfilling the Fifth Commandment, *Thou shall not murder*, would be a freebie—like the middle square of the bingo card, one we can all just cross off right away. But Luther teaches that fulfilling the Fifth Commandment requires more than just not killing people. Luther teaches that *Thou shall not murder* means that "we are to love and fear God, so that we neither endanger nor harm the lives of our neighbors, but instead help and support them in all of life's needs." Do no harm *and* support others in all their needs.

Likewise, where sex is concerned, for sexual flourishing to occur we must be guided by more than just the absence of "no" and the absence of harm. That's why I believe we must also bring *concern* to our consent and mutuality. Concern moves us closer to the heart of Jesus' own ethic:

love God and our neighbor as ourselves. It requires us to act on another's behalf. It reframes the choice entirely outside of our own self-interest in a way that consent and mutuality alone do not.

Concern means taking notice of how our sexual behavior affects ourselves and each other. I may be having a mutually pleasurable, consensual relationship with someone, but if I am cheating on my spouse at the same time, I have failed to show concern for the person I am married to. If I am in a crisis and totally distraught, I may be more likely to consent to sex when in fact it is the last thing I need. If someone intuits this and sleeps with me anyway, they have consent, but they are not showing care and concern. A sexual ethic that includes concern means seeing someone as a whole person and not just a willing body.

The only way to show true concern for ourselves and others is to *see*, to pay attention. As the social philosopher and mystic Simone Weil said, "Attention is the rarest and purest form of generosity." Seeing ourselves and others more truly is what I'm inviting us to do as we forge a new Christian sexual ethic—one that's based not on a standardized list of *thou shall nots* but on concern for each other's flourishing.

I propose a sexual reformation for those who have been hurt. I also propose it for those who have done the hurting, for those who doubt my authority and those who are certain they know all there is to know about what God thinks of sex. It is time for us to grab some matches and haul our antiquated and harmful ideas about sex and bodies and gender into the yard. It's time to pay attention to what is happening to the people around us, and to our loved ones, and it's time for us to be concerned. And I'm not suggesting we make a few simple amendments; new wine in old skins ain't gonna cut it. I'm saying let's burn it the fuck down and start over. Because it's time.

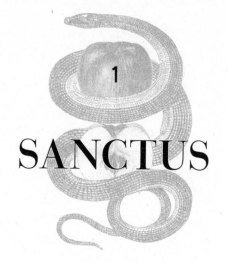

1

SANCTUS

"Can you pray for me?"

The text message, with a teary-faced emoji, flashed across my phone as I got in my car and drove to the place where I was scheduled to preach in an hour. I called my parishioner Cecilia back, knowing that she was likely to be in tears given the urgency of the text. As I merged onto the highway and dodged the slow drivers so prevalent now in Denver since we legalized weed, she told me—not for the first time—how brokenhearted she was after breaking up with her first-ever lover, James. She was thirty-one. And she was crushed.

Cecilia is one of dozens of young people in my congregation—and millions of people around the world—who were raised in the Evangelical "purity movement." She was taught to "wait for marriage" and told that if she wanted to lead a life pleasing to God, she must remain pure for her future husband. Like many other young women (but not young men, because they for some reason weren't asked), she has the "purity ring" to prove it—a ring she wore in her teens and twenties as a sign of her commitment to holiness.

Encouraging young people to not have sex until marriage is nothing new, but in 1997 a twenty-one-year-old preacher's kid named Joshua Harris wrote a book called *I Kissed Dating Goodbye*, in which he made the case that not going all the way before marriage was not going far enough. *True* purity, Harris posited, demands that you refrain from even kissing someone until you kiss your spouse at the wedding altar.*

But for Cecilia as for so many girls, that spouse never materialized. And when Cecilia was twenty-nine and had left conservative Christianity behind and taken her first lover, she had had no practice at it. She didn't know how to handle the pleasure and passion and connection and the amazing chemicals that wash over one's brain when that much skin and soul are exposed to another's. She assumed she was in love and that it would last forever, but then James cheated on her, and the relationship ended.

She wanted to forgive him, but this was not the first problem in their relationship. It had been hard for her to not be freaked out when her boyfriend first talked about having a sexual past. Him cheating on her only made her more insecure.

"Nadia, it's stupid, I know, but honestly, it felt like he

---

* Harris concedes now that some of his ideas were misguided, and he is currently on a bit of an apology tour. See his website, www.joshharris.com.

was an expert and I was a novice," she said through her waning tears. "Even though he tried to convince me otherwise, I felt so inadequate."

I thought, *You were robbed*. The church took away over a decade of her sexual development. All this time, she could have been gaining the kind of wisdom that comes from making her own choices, from having lovers, from making mistakes, from falling in love.

I could hear a deep inhale and exhale on the phone before she went on. "My friend suggested that I could get over this pain by just screwing around with other guys, so I did that. But last night I slept with someone random and it was awful and now I feel like shit, even though I don't think it's, like, *morally* wrong."

I took my exit off I-70 and told Cecilia I agreed. At this juncture, casual sex probably wasn't her path to healing. "You're exposing so much surface area of yourself with these encounters," I said, "so maybe that means there's more of you to get hurt. Now you know," I said, my heart aching for Cecilia. "There's nothing wrong with any of this."

"I'm so mad I wasn't told any of this earlier," she said, with a mix of betrayal and even rage in her voice. "I'm so angry."

I was, too. But I told her the same thing that keeps running through my head regarding what the church has taught about sex: that being mad is understandable and necessary, but its usefulness is limited. This was her story. It was *hers*. She could claim it, and then move on to what was next instead of staying stuck. She may not have been able to choose what happened to her, but she did get to choose what it was going to *mean*.

"Thanks. I'll grab you at church tomorrow, so maybe you could say a prayer over me?" she said before hanging up.

The next day, Sunday, I stood among my congregation as my colleague Reagan presided at the communion table. On my hands, I could smell the spicy myrrh from where I had just made a sign of the cross on Cecilia's forehead, a sensual moment when my thumb traced the sign of the cross over her and the fragrance of the oil filled the space around us. I held Cecilia's hands in mine, and her tears spilled over them as I prayed that God would guide her and bring her wisdom and integrate all the parts of herself—mental, spiritual, sexual, physical—so that she would feel whole. After all, the Greek word for salvation is *sozo*, which means "to heal, bring wholeness, preserve." This is what God does. God heals fractured parts of ourselves back together into wholeness.

Moments after anointing Cecilia, I looked over at Reagan, with his bright blue eyes, barrel chest, and trim beard. He stood behind the table where two hundred of us had gathered to proclaim our faith through bread, wine, song. He lifted his hands, singing:

> *We join with saints and angels*
> *in the chorus of praise*
> *that rings through eternity*
> *lifting our voices to magnify you as we sing . . .*

· · ·

And Reagan's one voice became many as the four-part harmony of the gathered people rushed into the space that his lone voice never could have filled. You can't sing harmony alone. Harmony is a sound of unity in difference, a sound of one thing that is possible only when people who differ from each other unite. *E pluribus unum.*

> *Holy holy holy Lord,*
> *God of power and might,*
> *Heaven and earth are filled with your glory.*
> *Hosanna in the highest.*

The scent of myrrh on my hands now mixed with the incense burning on the altar—frankincense rising up to God like a prayer—and I wondered about this holiness of which we sing, and which the church has equated to purity, sexual and otherwise. I don't doubt that the primary reason the church obsesses over sexual "purity" is, at its heart, noble: we want to be holy, to experience sanctity. But what *is* holiness?

Holiness is the union we experience with one another and with God. Holiness is when more than one become one, when what is fractured is made whole. Singing in harmony. Breastfeeding a baby. Collective bargaining. Dancing. Admitting our pain to someone, and hearing them say, "Me, too." Holiness happens when we are integrated as physical, spiritual, sexual, emotional, and political beings. Holiness is

---

* Franz Schubert's *Deutsche Messe.*

the song that has always been sung, perhaps even the sound that was first spoken when God said, "Let there be light."

And holiness was my prayer for Cecilia. But holiness is not something we earn, or create, or strive to become. It's not about self-improvement. It's just something we bump up against by happenstance, something that jars us into ourselves and out of ourselves at the same time. Holiness happens in those moments when we are blissfully free from our ego and yet totally connected to our self and something else. It is in the smell of a newborn's head and the exhaustion of a laboring mother. The moment during a celebration when you are sharing a cake with those you love, and you take the first bite and every pleasure sensor is firing *holy holy holy*. Holiness is the thing I never saw coming that makes me catch my breath because I know the sacred has interrupted my isolation.

And—I insist on this—when two loving individuals, two bearers of God's image, are unified in an erotic embrace, there is space for something holy. What was separate has come together. Two spirits, two bodies, two stories are drawn so close that they are something together that they cannot be alone. There is unity.

During the autumn when I first started really thinking about all these issues around sex and the church, I called a close friend from the road. He is not a Christian, but I asked, with an unwarranted urgency, "Why do you think it is that the church has tried to control human sexuality so much throughout the ages?"

He answered, "I guess I always assumed the church saw sex as its competition."

The moment he said it, I knew it was at least partially true. Sex does compete with the church. Sex, like religion, can alleviate the pain of separateness. It can soothe the ache of not being seen. It can tame the fear of insignificance. It can circumvent the lacerating experience of feeling incomplete.

Whether we realize it or not, we often find ways to alleviate feelings of existential aloneness through the seeking of unity. We fill our lives with things that distract us from the sound of our deepest isolation tapping at the window. Food, entertainment, success, sex, relationships, busyness, gossip—there are plenty of ways to divert our attention from the unavoidable, terrifying aloneness of human existence.

But there is a difference between *distraction from* and *alleviation of.* Moments of unity—holiness—actually alleviate isolation, which is not the same as simply distracting us from our isolation. In the same way, smoking cigarettes and drinking coffee distract from the feelings of hunger, but eating food alleviates them. Temporarily, of course. But that is what it means to be human.

In religion specifically, we seek alleviation of this existential aloneness via union with God and union with others who are seeking the same thing. We pray for the concerns of others. We stand around tables of bread and wine. We join with saints and angels singing the chorus of praise that rings through eternity: *holy holy holy.*

Reagan once told me that he always lifts his eyes to heaven as he sings the *holy holy holy.* It's a way of acknowledging that his voice is one of millions that have joined, are joining, and always will join with the heavens to sing of God. It reminds him that he is a creature endowed with a life and soul through the very breath of God, the breath he uses to sing with angels and all the faithful. The boundaries of his separate self are for the moment vanquished, subsumed into an eternal song. *This* is holiness.

To connect to the holy is to access the deepest, juiciest part of our spirits. Perhaps this is why we set up so many boundaries, protections, and rules around both sex and religion. Both pursuits expose such a large surface area of the self, which can then be either hurt or healed. But when the boundaries, protections, and rules become more important than the sacred thing they are intended to protect, casualties ensue.

But no matter how much we strive for purity in our minds, bodies, spirits, or ideologies, purity is not the same as holiness. It's just easier to define what is pure than what is holy, so we pretend they are interchangeable.

In the late eighteenth century, the temperance movement was founded to combat a serious social ill: excessive alcohol consumption. The industrial revolution and a rapid increase in migration had led to more and more people living in crowded urban environments, causing a sudden alienation from many established social structures. This change (along with a glut of newly imported molasses, which allowed for new types of hard alcohol to be more widely available) saw with it an increase in drunkenness, especially among men. Excessive drinking was creating havoc in the home and workplace. Domestic violence and absenteeism ate away at the health and security of so many people's lives. So some concerned wives, mothers, and ministers started a movement to encourage the moderation of alcohol consumption. There was a fracturing that needed to be addressed.*

But something happened that seems to happen in all movements eventually—a split between moderates and extremists. For the extremists, tempering the consumption of alcohol didn't go far enough—temperance wasn't pure enough, didn't treat the evil of alcohol as evil enough. So onto the stage of American moral drama walked the abstinence movement, which argued that alcohol in any amount is evil and must be avoided entirely for the sake of individual and societal well-being.

I grew up in a religious tradition that eschewed all alcohol consumption—a practice that is called "teetotaling," which I always took to mean that *tea* was the *totality* of what we were allowed to drink. But actually, the term came from rallies that the prohibition purists held in opposition to their morally soft counterparts in the temperance movement. Large canvas signs with a capital *T* for "total abstinence" hung above the stage at rallies, announcing the beliefs of the purists. So a moral war cry, and not the consumption of Earl Grey, was the origin of the term "teetotaler." Regardless, what interests me is how the "that isn't going far enough" instinct that so many humans have, the instinct for purity, shows up in movements and religions of all sorts.

---

* According to the PBS documentary series *Prohibition*, by Ken Burns and Lynn Novick, http://www.pbs.org/kenburns/prohibition.

Sure, there are times in which taking the middle path is a foolish half-measure. (I say this as someone who struggled with alcoholism and now has twenty-six years of complete sobriety; the middle path is not available to me, and I know it.) But I wonder how different the story of our country would have been if temperance, instead of abstinence, had been allowed to take hold. We will never know, because in a short amount of time, enough people were so enflamed by the "moderation is not going far enough" rhetoric of the teetotalers that the course of our nation's laws and history would forever be marked by it. The abstinence movement was led, by the way, by Baptists and Methodists, who would have considered Jesus himself, with all his wine drinking, too impure for their Christian movement. They convinced every major Protestant group in America to sign on to their more-pure-than-temperance prohibition movement. (Well, all Protestants except Lutherans, who weren't about to part with their beer, and Episcopalians, who couldn't see the point of life without sherry.)

The religiosity of the prohibition movement was stoked by a genuine desire to lead holy lives pleasing to God. But purity is easier to regulate than holiness.

And regulate they did. Getting churches and individuals and civic groups to sign on to abstinence from alcohol was not enough. Eventually there was a push in the schools. The prohibition movement ensured that teetotalist textbooks made their way into elementary schools all across the country. Many American schoolchildren attended abstinence classes several times a week, where instructors warned them that even one drink of alcohol could burn the throat and ruin the lining of the stomach. Alcohol caused deafness and lunacy in drinkers' children and even grandchildren, they said. Drinking was known to lead to spontaneous combustion.

It's bizarre to think of how far prohibition went—or maybe not, given that similar fear-mongering would soon be used to target sex. (Like, even kissing your girlfriend leads to sex, and sex outside marriage leads to disease and death, so you'd better kiss dating goodbye.) But so strong was the scapegoating of alcohol for every wrong, injustice, and problem in society that the "that's not going far enough" crowd eventually thought, "Getting (almost) every denomination to sign on isn't going far enough, and just getting our values promoted in schools and scaring the bejesus out of children isn't going far enough . . . fuck it, *let's amend the U.S. Constitution!*"

They amended the U.S. Constitution!

But here's the problem with capital *T* total abstinence: when our country made drinking illegal and instilled fear in children about the evils of alcohol, it led, not to an increase of holiness, but to a culture of secrecy, hypocrisy, and double standards. I am fairly certain that the surge in organized crime and black market activity in the United States during prohibition would not have happened had we not insisted on a uniform idea of purity for the entire country.

We all want to remain safe and healthy. But fast food in America does more harm to the health of our people than almost anything else, and good Lord, I'm not about to suggest we amend the Constitution to ban chicken nuggets. I can only imagine what kind of black market would sprout up were we to make junk food illegal.

The desire to live a holy life that is pleasing to God is understandable, but this desire is also fraught with pitfalls.

Our purity systems, even those established with the best of intentions, do not make us holy.* They only create insiders and outsiders. They are mechanisms for delivering our drug of choice: self-righteousness, as juice from the fruit of the tree of knowledge of good and evil runs down our chins. And these purity systems affect far more than our relationship to sex and booze: they show up in political ideology, in the way people shame each other on social media, in the way we obsess about "eating clean." Purity most often leads to pride or to despair, not to holiness. Because holiness is about union *with*, and purity is about separation *from*.

J esus seemed to want connection with those around him, not separation. He touched human bodies deemed unclean as if they were themselves holy: dead little girls, lepers, menstruating women. People of his day were disgusted that Jesus' disciples would eat with unwashed hands, and they tried to shame him for it. But he responded, "It is not what enters the mouth that makes one unclean but what comes out of it that defiles." He was loyal to the law, just not at the expense of the people.

Jesus kept violating boundaries of decency to get to the people on the other side of that boundary, those who'd been wounded by it, those who were separated from the others:

---

* The term "purity systems" refers to ways in which Christians often seek holiness through moralism and is in no way referring to other religions and their practices.

the motherless, the sex workers, the victims, and the victimizers. He cared about real holiness, the connection of things human and divine, the unity of sinners, the coming together of that which was formerly set apart.

When I think of holiness, the kind that is sensual and embodied and free from shame and deeply present in the moment and comes from union with God, I think of a particular scene in the Gospels when, right in the middle of a dinner party, a woman cracks open a jar of myrrh and pours it over Jesus' feet. She then takes her unbound hair and wipes his feet, mixing her mane, her tears, and her offering on the feet of God. Her separateness, from herself and her God, is alleviated in that moment. Holiness braided the strands of her being into their original and divine integrated configuration.

And those in the room with the woman and Jesus did what we humans too often do. They turned their backs on the holiness and intimacy of what they were witnessing, and instead accused Jesus of impurity.

I thought of that woman as I anointed Cecilia that night at church. I thought of the transgressive sensuality of a woman cracking open a jar of costly perfume, the scent of myrrh filling the room as her tears fell on the feet of the savior of the whole world.

Holy holy holy Lord,
God of power and might,
Heaven and earth are filled with your glory.
Hosanna in the highest.

THE FIRST BLESSING

IN OUR BEGINNING, God was maybe bored and a little lonely, so God created a terrifyingly vast universe, which included the earth. The earth, our speck of life, was just a void, and this great nothingness was super dark. Before creation, all there was was God, so in order to bring the world into being, God had to kind of scoot over. To bring the world into being, God chose to take up less space— you know, to make room.

So before God spoke the world into being, God scooted over. God wanted to share. Like the kind-faced woman on the subway who takes her handbag onto her lap so that there's room for you to sit next to her. She didn't have to do it, but that's just who she is; the kind-faced subway lady's nature is that she makes room for others.

And the kind-faced subway lady could have made this universe in any manner she chose—she could have brought the universe into existence fully formed—but she's a gardener by nature, so she grew it from seed, knowing it was going to be a process. And the first seeds came in the form of four words from the mouth of God.

Let there be light.

God's words do what they say. So, from the breath of God, the world came into being. Bang! Oceans, land, heavens, sun, moon, stars, plants, and things called sea monsters.*

It all took some time. It was a process, and a strangely collaborative one at that. Rather than God doing everything, God shared the work with creation. Calling the earth to bring forth vegetation and the seas to bring forth sea monsters. God was obsessed with the idea of seeds, and made a self-sustaining system inside of the life God was creating. Like Russian nesting dolls of life. Inside of life makes more life.

Then God had an absolute explosion of creativity and made animals. Amoebas. Chickens. Crickets. Orangutans. And God blessed them by saying "Be fruitful and multiply."

The very first blessing was sex.

Then God said, "Let us create humans in our own image and likeness."

Wait . . . who exactly is God talking to? Was God talking to all the animals? Was God talking to Jesus and the Holy Spirit? Was God talking to God's self in the first-person plural? Hard to say.

God the community, God the family, God the friend group, God the opposite of isolation, said, "Let's do this together. Let's create humanity in our image and likeness. Let there be us and them in one being."

Male and female God created them.

God created every one of us in the male and female image of God. God gave us something so holy that it could never be harmed, never be taken from us: God's image. A source code of grace. A never-aloneness. Our origin and destination: God.

---

* Genesis 1:20.

2

BUILD-A-BEAR

Do you not believe that you are [each] an Eve? The
sentence of God on this sex of yours lives on even
in our times and so it is necessary that the guilt
should live on, also. You are the one who opened
the door to the Devil, you are the one who first
plucked the fruit of the forbidden tree, you are the
first who deserted the divine law; you are the one
who persuaded him whom the Devil was not strong
enough to attack. All too easily you destroyed the
image of God, man. Because of your desert, that is,
death, even the Son of God had to die.

—Tertullian (second-century Christian theologian),
The Apparel of Women

The year my daughter Harper turned ten, she built a teddy
bear. For, like, $80.

The next morning at breakfast, I watched as she placed
her sparkly blue Build-a-Bear, which she had sensibly dressed

in a white tank top that featured a rhinestone heart, on our kitchen bar. She leaned it against the wall, where it stayed for weeks and accompanied her every morning as she ate.

I don't know what it is about eating cereal that makes Harper zone out. But ever since she was little I've watched her in the kitchen of our small brick home, when the morning light of the Colorado sun shines unwelcomingly bright on her face, as she shovels cornflakes into her mouth and gazes into who knows what, lost in her glorious girl thoughts. I love watching her.

One morning, a week after she made her own teddy bear, Harper took a bite of her cereal and asked between crunches what the bumps were on her chest. Her body was doing what young growing bodies do, yet I was suddenly afraid for her. She was ten, and things don't always go well for girls who develop early. To have a female body at all is to be a walking risk, and I feared for my daughter's girl body with its own little rhinestone heart.

The year that a grown man masturbated in front of me and two other girls outside a candy shop in Colorado Springs was the same year a boy kissed me for the first time. I was twelve.

The hallway of our just-built church still had the new-car smell of carpet adhesive and hope. The carpet was only a few months old by the time I stood on it in 1981, my back held against the textured gray Sheetrock, with the preacher's son pressed against me, the smells of his breath and the hallway mingling in my nostrils.

For the first time in my life I was feeling the attention of a boy. A boy! That distant and powerful population. The ruling class, the eternal upperclassmen, the ones for whom everything existed. Including me.

To be a young Christian girl in the early 1980s in Colorado Springs was to know a lot about place, order, rank, and currency. Outside the church, American society had begun to pay lip service to equality—even allowing women to have credit cards in their own names!—but the community I was raised in still wanted women kept in their proper place. They claimed that the Garden of Eden story, our origin story, demanded it.* It's hard to call something sexist bullshit when every authority figure in your life tells you the Bible declares it is "God's will."

The message I received was that when Eve emerged from Adam's rib, she entered life grateful to be a helper. She was only ever an "us," never once an "I." God gave her to Adam, like a mail-order bride. Adam was her purpose.

And now, as a skinny twelve-year-old girl with the attention of *a boy*, I, too, had purpose. I was worthy. I was finally going to be Eve to an Adam.

I could usually be found at church flanked by Christie Waters and Charlotte Perkins, two of the prettiest girls there,

---

* To my point that how we interpret the Garden of Eden story matters, *Malleus Maleficarum* (*Hammer of Witches*), a fifteenth-century document, draws heavily on Genesis 3 and provided the Inquisition its principal theological justification for persecuting women as witches. In the decades following its publication, thousands of women were executed.

who kept me around mostly because I was funny and a good listener. Christie had perfectly feathered blond hair and wore white turtlenecks dotted with tiny hearts or stars or sailboats under her brightly colored crewneck sweaters. Then there was Charlotte. Charlotte was so pretty and sweet. Olive-skinned, tenderhearted, and shockingly curvy for a twelve-year-old. Of course I envied both of them.

The delayed arrival of my own curves was made even more distressing by how thin I had become.* I was all limbs and bone and acerbic humor. So while Charlotte and Christie got all the attention, I just made fun of the boys who gave it to them, until one day during church when the attention fell on me.

A note from Alan, the eldest son of the preacher, showed up in my lap. I stopped pretending to pay attention to the sermon long enough to look over and make sure the note was not for Charlotte or Christie. I pointed at myself doubtfully. He smiled and nodded.

"Hi," was all the note said.

"Hi," I wrote back, cautious.

For three thrilling weeks, Alan turned his eyes to me. He'd pass me small folded notes as we sat on the beige-cushioned pew with the other church kids, trying to get through the forty-minute sermon. The prayer request cards (PRCs, we called them) and golf pencils, nested in racks on the back of the pew in front of us, were the only things we were allowed access to in worship other than our Bibles.

---

* Due to an autoimmune disorder, Graves' disease, which I wrote about in *Pastrix: The Cranky, Beautiful Faith of a Sinner and Saint* (New York: Jericho Books, 2013).

We drew on PRCs, made tiny airplanes out of them, passed notes scribbled onto them. They were our only resource, bland as manna but still enough to make do.

I became acutely aware of where Alan was sitting at church, and when he was looking my way. Like the background from a photo with a single point of focus, the edges of everything that was not Alan began to blur around him. Once Alan sat right next to me and caressed my arm with his hand for a moment during prayer. His fingers slowly and gently traced my skinny triceps, pulling on my insides like a church bell.

Whenever I got dressed for church, I wondered which dress Alan might think was cute. And I thought of how Charlotte looked in her Sunday dresses and I longed for a more womanly form. I had never before thought of another person when I chose what to wear. I had been a girl unbothered by clothes, but now my clothes and my hair and my skin had a purpose: they were the basis on which I would be evaluated as being worthy of desire, the main currency girls had at their disposal. We were not being "lifted up" as leaders or praised for our bravery. We were being instructed on how to make the most of our attractiveness. That, and perhaps niceness and quietness, was the only thing we had going for us.

That same year, Charlotte, Christie, and I, along with all the other twelve- and thirteen-year-old girls, went to church every Tuesday night for Christian Charm class. For an hour each week, women from the church would instruct us on important matters like nail polish, how to stand, how to sit, how to talk, when to talk, what colors looked best on us, how to apply makeup, et cetera. They took our measurements before and after the ten-week course, measuring the progress we'd made toward weight loss via the calorie chart inside our *Christian Charm* workbook. (It was printed, helpfully, opposite the Bible reading chart.) "Femininity," the workbook explained, was my "crowning glory: purity, a clean heart, sweetness, a quiet spirit, modesty, chastity, a demure manner."

No low-cut shirts were allowed in Christian Charm class. Nothing suggestive. "Boys are stimulated visually," was the perennial message. "You must help them not give in to lust." At the same time, we were taught that we must make ourselves look as pretty as possible. *Boys like pretty. But don't be sexy. Unless you're married. Then you can be sexy. But only to your husband.*

And don't forget to cultivate that quiet spirit.

I look back on those classes with a mix of disgust and tenderness. The women who taught them were perpetuating a pernicious system of female submission and male domination. And yet, if all we girls had was this one form of currency, perhaps it was also generous and protective for older women to help us know how to make the most of it. As one of the girls who needed the most help—getting the lowest score in the *Christian Charm* workbook's "How Feminine Am I?" quiz*—I was grateful for the guidance. My biting comments about the boys who paid attention to my prettier, curvier friends were just a smokescreen covering the desperate envy I felt toward them, because they were

---

* My favorite comic book, *Bitch Planet* by Kelly Sue DeConnik, used this very workbook as source material for its Compliance Manual. See https://imagecomics.com/comics/series/bitch-planet.

rich in the currency of being attractive. I wanted to be considered pretty like them, to be worthy of desire. I still do.

That summer, Christie, Charlotte, and I walked to the strip mall candy store in search of chocolate bars and Twizzlers, but it was closed. We stood there squinting in the bright July sun, trying to figure out where the next-closest place to buy candy was, when in a low voice Christie said, "Um, you guys . . . ," and motioned for us to look in the corner of the courtyard.

At first I didn't understand what I was looking at. Why in the world did that man have a long coat on in this heat? Then I saw. I looked at my friends. They saw, too. We froze for a long moment, not knowing what to do, before running all the way back to my house as fast as we could, unsure whether the man would follow us. Sweat and Love's Baby Soft lotion stung my eyes as my Nikes hit the pavement.

I felt a wrongness in my body that day. Something like the caution I felt in my gut when I received my first note from Alan, but fuller and more searing. Like a stranger had trapped something inside of me by showing me a part of his body that I never wanted to see.

"What did you *say*?" my older sister, Barbara, asked when later that day I told her what happened. We sat on her lumpy antique bed and I tried to seem older than I was, to make it seem like I didn't care. And when I replied, "Nothing," the trapped thing burrowed deeper.

. . .

"Meet me in the hall by the fourth-grade class after the closing prayer," the final note from Alan read. And later, on the way home, after I'd met him in the hall and he'd pressed me against the wall, I could still taste his salt on my mouth.

Every seat of our Chevy station wagon was full on the drive home, which was not unusual. At church, my mom would invite any Air Force Academy cadet she could find to come eat lasagna and spend Sunday afternoon at our house. My dad was on the academy faculty and my parents headed the cadet ministry at church, so our dining room table was more often than not full of clean-cut, exceedingly polite college kids, usually young men.

In the car that day, my lanky, twelve-year-old body was wedged between two cadets in the middle back seat as another cadet drove. I tasted Alan on my mouth, and my secret transgression felt palpable. Did the cadets beside me know what I'd just done? I could think of nothing else but Alan; every edge was blurred. A boy had desired to press his lips to mine. I'd done it. I had attracted him. He'd considered me worthy.

So I hadn't been paying attention to the cadets' conversation, lost as I was in the taste of a boy, when the sound of my friend's name snapped me to attention.

From the front seat, I heard the driver casually comment, "Charlotte has become quite the . . . buxom young woman," and the other men in the car nodded, chuckled, and looked over me at each other knowingly.

"Man, no kidding," the cadet to my right added.

How the topic of another twelve-year-old girl's breasts possibly could have come up and been received as an acceptable topic of conversation, I have no idea. All I know is that my beautiful, prematurely curvy friend Charlotte's body was being considered, discussed, and evaluated by four men while I sat there trying to have a demure, quiet spirit, trying to pretend I hadn't noticed or didn't mind. But I did mind. When I heard grown men discuss Charlotte's body with a tone that seriously differed from how they might've discussed mine, my disgust mixed uncomfortably with envy. I folded my arms over my flat chest.

When we got home, I walked up the half stairway of our 1960s split-level to my bedroom and threw up in my mildly rusted Holly Hobby wastepaper basket.

Thirty years later, the day after my ten-year-old daughter asked what the bumps on her chest were, I watched again as she sat in her cereal-eating daze in our kitchen. But on that day, she stopped for a moment and stared at her light blue bear without blinking. Then she got up, grabbed two square yellow Post-it notes from the stack on the end table, balled them up, and placed them under the white tank top of her shiny blue bear, one on the right and one under the rhinestone heart on the left. She sat back down without a word and finished her cereal.

When girls develop, especially when they develop early, they begin trading in a currency they probably don't yet want and definitely don't yet understand. They remain girls and yet quickly and by no fault of their own become objects for inspection and desire. Sadly, most of the women I know who developed early were called sluts.

That morning in my kitchen, I panicked. I feared Harper would soon join the host of women before her, becoming an object for the desire or disgust of others. But I didn't want my daughter's body to be placed in the great worthiness sorting system. I wanted her to remain free in her body, unbothered by its attractiveness, unbothered by fear of harassment or assault, unbothered by the gaze of men. I wanted her to relax in the inherent dignity of her body, to be at home in it like the gift of God that it is.

And as I feared for her and hoped for her and watched her give a teddy bear tiny breasts, my thoughts turned to my friend Charlotte for maybe the first time in thirty years. I grabbed my phone, opened Facebook, entered "Charlotte Perkins" in the search field, and learned that at the age of thirty-eight she had died of breast cancer.

As I write this book, our country is in the midst of an upheaval, or what I would call the #MeToo apocalypse.

In Greek, the word *apocalypse* means "to uncover, to peel away, to show what's underneath." The manner in which some men comment on, threaten, masturbate in front of, intimidate, and assault female bodies is finally being brought out of the dark ubiquity of women's personal experience and into the light of public discourse. Each day, women endure male acts of dominance in countless ways. When a woman is forced to either laugh at dirty jokes made by the men in her workplace or face social or professional repercussions, it is an act of domination. When a man stands over a woman, taking up her physical space, explaining something to her she already knows, it is physically reminding her of how easily dominated she is; it is a reminder of her place. When a man corners three little girls outside a candy store, opens his coat, and masturbates in front of them, it is not so much about sexual proclivity as it is about power. The thing making that man erect is his assertion of dominance.

The corner has peeled up on our culture, and now there is a little cat fur and dust on it, and we can't get it to stick back down. I suggest we must take that peeled-up corner and pull, even if it hurts.

If we look as deep as we can stomach, what we will find at the center is heresy. The nineteenth-century theologian Friedrich Schleiermacher defines *heresy* as "that which preserves the *appearance* of Christianity, and yet contradicts its *essence*."*

The heresy is this: with all the trappings of Christianity behind us, we who seek to justify or maintain our dominance over another group of people have historically used the Bible, Genesis in particular, to prove that domination is not actually an abuse of power at the expense of others, but is indeed part of "God's plan."†

Genesis is an origin story, and every culture has its own.

---

* And there you have the appearance of Christianity (Bible verses and God-talk) contradicting its essence (love God, and love your neighbor as yourself).

† Other systems of domination that have been asserted as "God's Plan" by those who benefit from them include: slavery, segregation, and their modern-day counterpart, mass incarceration.

Origin stories tell us how the world came about, where we came from, and other important things like why snakes don't have legs. We may think we know our own origin story really well, but the Garden of Eden account in Genesis is notably devoid of several elements that lore has inserted into it. For instance, there actually are no mentions of original sin, "a fall from grace," Satan, or temptation. And there wasn't even an apple involved.

But there's a reason we think of original sin and apples and temptation and a fall from grace when we think about Genesis. It's because a guy named Augustine interpreted it that way.

Augustine was a North African bishop and theologian from the fourth century whose writings have deeply influenced Christian thinking to this day. The world around him was changing, and he himself was changing, so like many of us, he looked to scripture for guidance. His own version of the Garden of Eden story goes like this: God created paradise for humans to live in, but Eve messed it up for everyone by eating a piece of fruit that God told her not to eat, and this caused a fall from grace. So now all of humanity is cursed, and this so-called original sin of Eve's became sort of, I don't know . . . a sexually transmitted disease. According to Augustine, every person born after Eve inherited her original sin, and so it is essential that men should be dominant—controlling women so they don't screw over humanity any more than they already have.

It is important to know, as we consider the origin of the church's beliefs about sex and bodies and gender, that

Augustine's theology and interpretation of Bible stories were rooted in his own shame. Augustine felt shame about his own sexual proclivities and regret about his licentious behavior before converting to Christianity.*

Augustine's shame reportedly took root when, as an adolescent, he got an erection while at a Roman bath. Embarrassing, yes. But Augustine was so consumed with the shame of not being able to control his erections that he spent a decade writing a theological treatise. In the treatise, he set out to prove that the main condition of paradise before the fall was that Adam could control his erections with his own will. Then Eve messed everything up.

I feel for him. Augustine, like all of us, had *issues*. And it was more than fine for him to take his own concerns into the creative project of biblical interpretation. He is allowed, just like we all are.

But we must stop confusing his baggage and our baggage and our pastors' baggage and our parents' baggage with God's will. Because while many of Augustine's teachings have been revered for generations, when it came to his ideas around sex and gender, he basically took a dump and the church encased it in amber. But instead of realizing this was one guy's personal shit, we assumed it was straight from God. We ignored the harmful impact these teachings have on actual people, and the way they've contributed to the sexual misconduct that we are becoming increasingly aware

---

* "How St. Augustine Invented Sex" by Stephen Greenblatt (*The New Yorker,* June 19, 2017).

of. Because when it comes down to it, the issue behind most sexual harassment and misconduct is one of male dominance, the kind that religion often tells us is "God's will."

Tertullian, another one of the early church's most influential theologians, interpreted the Eden story as saying that women destroyed the *imago dei*—the image of God—in men. He also believed, as the quote that opened this chapter indicates, that women are to blame for the death of Jesus. Because of this, he wrote, it is "God's will" that men exert dominance over women.

This is why I welcome our current apocalypse. As a mother of a (now) teenage girl, I welcome this moment of cultural uncovering, because we need to see just how deep the heresy of male domination runs.

And as a mother of a teenage boy, I feel that we must also look at the ways in which men, too, have been harmed by the heresy of male dominance.

Recently, a friend of mine surprised me with a copy of *Man in Demand*, the male counterpart to the *Christian Charm* workbook for girls, written by the same author (along with her husband, of course). I had no idea it even existed, but right there in its eighty poorly illustrated pages were the instructions for manhood. Page after page devoted to building confidence and learning God's plan for your life, a plan that included having impeccable manners, an assertive walk, and a masculine hairstyle. I began to understand why in so many of the interviews I've conducted with my male parishioners, queer and straight alike, they spoke about the shame they felt simply for being who they were: too creative, too soft, too quiet. Not dominant.

But I am not satisfied with just naming the harm that religious teachings have done and leaving it at that. These creation stories are *ours*. And if the church has used them to justify the harm, let them now be used to heal. If those who came before us looked to Genesis to find a justification for domination, we can look to Genesis to find a justification for its opposite: dignity.

Genesis says,

> God created humankind in God's image,
> in the image of God he created them;
> male and female he created them.

All human beings are made in the male and female (not male *or* female) image and likeness of God, and God went so far as to have a human body and walk among us as Jesus. I believe this is what allows us all to absolutely reject domination and insist on its opposite: dignity.

Being bearers of God's image allows us to insist on the self-determination of our bodies and our pleasure and our hearts, and it compels us to insist on the self-determination of the same for others. It allows us to call out and reject harassment, assault, the sexualization of children, and every other thing that compromises the inherent dignity of human bodies.

Dignity, the quality or state of being worthy, comes from our origin, not from our efforts. Many of us learned from church that we become worthy through being pretty and having a quiet spirit if we are a girl, or being confident and a strong leader if we are a boy; we tried to mold ourselves and our behavior and our weight and our hairstyles and our facial expressions and our personalities into the shape we thought God wants us to have.* As if we could earn what has already been given to us.

Tertullian's flaccid interpretation of creation goes wrong in a very basic way: the *imago dei* cannot be harmed, much less removed. What a weak view of God, to suggest that the very image of God could be destroyed. I'm sorry, Tertullian, but women are not that powerful. Neither are men. And neither is the system of male domination and sexual harassment, nor a charm class where twelve-year-old girls have to take their measurements and learn how to remain silent.

---

* *Man in Demand* and the *Christian Charm* workbook both included pages dedicated to what facial expressions were Christian, what hairstyles were Christian, and what type of posture was Christian.

How Feminine am I?

Do my "feminine" qualities outnumber my "unfeminine" qualities? (Check list below.)

THESE DESTROY FEMININITY - THESE INCREASE FEMININITY

- ☐ A bulky, flabby figure....A trim, disciplined body ☐
- ☐ Sluggishness...............................Vitality ☐
- ☐ An unkempt appearance.............Careful grooming ☐
- ☐ Mannish attire.............Dainty, pretty clothing ☐
- ☐ Older, daring styles....Youthful, girlish styles ☐
- ☐ Revealing clothes................Modesty in dress ☐
- ☐ Over-display in dress....Quiet, conservative dress ☐
- ☐ Gawdy makeup....................."Natural" makeup ☐
- ☐ Mannish, short hairdos............Soft, clean hair ☐
- ☐ A dead-pan face.....................A ready smile ☐
- ☐ Tobacco odors................A delicate fragrance ☐
- ☐ Stained fingers............Clean, lovely hands ☐
- ☐ Smoking cigarettes........Abstaining from tobacco ☐
- ☐ Drinking liquor............Abstaining from liquor ☐
- ☐ Telling off-color jokes..............Clean speech ☐
- ☐ Reading smutty books.......Purity of thought life ☐
- ☐ An ungainly walk..........A lovely, graceful walk ☐
- ☐ Sprawling in chairs..............Sitting prettily ☐
- ☐ A slouching posture..........A queen-like posture ☐
- ☐ A loud" mouth...............Soft, gentle speech ☐
- ☐ Raspy gravelly voice........Pleasant vocal tones ☐
- ☐ Slangy expressions...........A refined vocabulary ☐
- ☐ Malicious gossip.....................A kind tongue ☐
- ☐ Swearing and profanity........A reverent attitude ☐
- ☐ A quarrelsome spirit....A peace-loving disposition ☐
- ☐ Explosive behavior....................Self-control ☐
- ☐ Domineering attitudes.....Thoughtfulness of others ☐
- ☐ Boisterous rowdiness............Ladylike reserve ☐
- ☐ False sophistication.....Sincerity and naturalness ☐
- ☐ Holding grudges..........Forgiving and forgetting ☐
- ☐ Over-display of self.....Dignity and self-respect ☐
- ☐ Dishonorable actions.........Unblemished integrity ☐
- ☐ Becoming "cheap".................Honor and virtue ☐
- ☐ Pessimism...............................Optimism ☐
- ☐ Conceit and vanity.........Modest self-confidence ☐
- ☐ Unchastity...........................Sexual purity ☐

_____ TOTAL   TOTAL _____

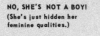

NO, SHE'S NOT A BOY!
(She's just hidden her
feminine qualities.)

Hunter, Emily. Christian Charm Course. *Eugene: Harvest House, 1985.*
Used with permission by Harvest House.

3

THIS SHIT IS FREE

The heart of True Love Waits is a personal, scriptural promise to God to be sexually abstinent from that day to one's wedding day. . . . Students who choose to order their lives after God's design experience the joy he intended. Those who do not live with the natural consequences of their choices: guilt, disease, broken hearts and relationships, damaged children, depression, and even death.

—Richard Ross, *True Love Waits Study Bible*

House for All Sinners and Saints was only a couple of years old when Stuart, the church drag queen (Shirley Delta Blow), suggested what has to be the most excellent congregational stewardship campaign of all time.

A small group of us sat together in my living room, discussing what stewardship might look like at HFASS. Technically the term "stewardship" refers to the responsibilities of someone who's been entrusted with something, but in practice it's just religious code for church fund-raising. We didn't know exactly how our church's campaign would look, but we knew that we were repelled by the way most congregations talk about money.

As we discussed this, Stuart spoke up: "Oh, I know!" We all looked at him, curious where this was leading.

"We'll make T-shirts," Stuart offered in his typically delightful manner. "On the front it will say 'This shit ain't free.' And on the back it will say 'So you better *tithe*, bitches!'"

When we were all finally breathing normally again, we sat around my coffee table eating chips and guac and talking honestly about the manipulative sermons we'd heard about giving money to the church. I piped up that the preacher at the Church of Christ I grew up in seemed to give a yearly sermon on the parable of the talents. He scared the snot out of everyone by claiming that all our money belongs to God, and if God comes back at the end of the world and finds out we haven't given back to God what is God's (meaning given it to the church), then it's basically some undefined punishment for us all.

Now that I have some distance from those heavy-handed sermons, I'm beginning to appreciate the spiritual practice of generosity. I've also begun to wonder if the parable might have something to say about our issue of sexual "purity."

The parable of the talents (Matthew 25:14–20) goes something like this. A rich dude gives away an absolute fortune ("talent" refers a *very* large sum of money and not, as you might think, the ability to juggle or tap-dance). He divides this treasure between three servants before leaving on a trip. And I find this little tidbit interesting: he gives a different amount to each of the servants according to their ability (*dynamis* in Greek, meaning "strength" or "capacity"), which, to me, denotes that people are different.

The first two servants see the giver of the gift as good and the gift as good, they invest it in ways that make it grow, and they flourish. But the third servant does something very different, mainly because the third servant has a troubling view of the rich guy. Even though the rich guy also generously entrusted the third servant with this amazing treasure, the servant is terrified of him, assuming him to be harsh and punishing. In his mind, the treasure isn't a gift; it's a trick.

So, too afraid to make decisions about the treasure, too afraid to take risks with it, the third servant digs a hole and buries it. Rather than using the treasure to discover how his own individual strength, capacity, and ability would come to life in the midst of such a gift, the third servant fearfully hides what was entrusted to him.

The master returns and congratulates the first two servants for what they have done with what he gave them, and they "enter into the joy of their master." But when he hears that the third servant buried the talent because he was afraid, he gets pretty pissed. The result: Outer darkness. Weeping. Teeth gnashing.

"I remember hearing a ton of sermons on this parable," I told the people in my living room that day. "It kind of felt like the preacher was parlaying a fearful view of God's judgment into an increase in tithing." (The moment the word "tithing" came out of my mouth, Stuart added, "Bitches!")

We are prone to manipulations like this because money is so often a place where we experience fear. Fear we won't have enough, fear we will never save enough to have that worry- and work-free retirement that is promised us in the American dream, fear that our life savings could be lost with a single cancer diagnosis. But money is also a place of shame. Shame about being poor, shame about being rich, shame for how little we give to charity, shame for how much we spend on coffee, shame about the amount of debt we carry. The more fear and shame we have about something, the more prone we are to manipulation—by the culture, by advertising, and especially by the church.

For many of us, sex is also rife with fear and shame. Fear of rejection, fear of loneliness, fear that we will never have a lover. Fear of exposing such a hurtable part of ourselves after being assaulted. Fear of being free and uninhibited. And then there's fear's sneaky brother, shame. Shame that we were sexually active at too young an age. Shame that we were virgins until we were thirty. Shame that we are in a sexless marriage. Shame that we don't really want sex with the kinds of people whom religion says we should want it with. Shame that sex doesn't interest us at all. Shame that we kind of want sex all the time.

As with money, there are a million ways the gift has morphed into a curse.

Recently, at Annie's Café on Colfax Avenue in Denver, I tried out on my parishioners Sara and Tim a term that was new for me. Tim is smooth-faced and fair, a bicycle

enthusiast, and Sara, a baker, has the big brown eyes and full cheeks that betray exactly what she must have looked like as a child. They were raised conservative Evangelicals, are twenty-nine and thirty-one, and have been married for three difficult years.

"You guys know stewardship, right?" I said out of the blue as we reviewed our menus. "I'm wondering about *sexual* stewardship. Is that a weird idea?"

"Nope," Tim answered, not even looking up from the menu. "I like it."

We talked for a while about work and family before our food came, and then I asked about what their church had taught them about sex and how that had affected them. Tim and Sara explained that they had been given something like a one-size-fits-all plan for how to date and how to be engaged.

The plan went something like this: If you're going to date someone (of the opposite gender, of course), don't "go too far" sexually. The plan seems simple in theory, but in practice it can be confusing. How far is "too far"? Nobody seems to exactly know the answer. And so dating becomes a constant tug-of-war between their desires and their fears. Buttons are undone and hastily redone as an afterthought. Body parts are touched and then quickly recoiled from, like a vampire from garlic. The fear of disappointing God and loved ones leads many unmarried Christian couples to resist their natural sexual attraction to each other.

Despite the confusing messages Tim and Sara received, they entered marriage confident they had been "obedient" to God, that they'd followed the plan. But now they're not so

sure that was the best idea. What they were taught wasn't—
and isn't—working for them.

Sex for Sara was at first incredibly painful, and for Tim
incredibly frustrating. They both felt inadequate, angry,
and confused, alternately blaming themselves and then each
other. They had been told that if they followed the rules,
they would have more satisfying and exciting sex than couples who'd had sex before marriage. The kind of sex that was
better because it was pure. But when they got married, they
found out that all of that was bullshit. The whole experience
was crushingly disappointing.

"I did everything right. I was a good girl," Sara recounted as she, Tim, and I shared a plate of french fries. "I
went to Bible college. And I didn't have sex until I was married. And . . . it didn't work." The problems in their bedroom quickly caused huge fights and seeped into every other
area of their life. Knowing their relationship was in trouble,
Sara turned to Christian books for women about how to
improve her marriage.

"Basically the books offered ways to manipulate your
husband by wearing lipstick and making sure you're cooking the kinds of dinner he likes," she said, shaking her head.
But Maybelline and a well-marbled steak didn't do the trick.

Tim was just as confused and desperate as she was. But
nothing worked. "Being a good Christian husband and the
spiritual head of the home was the only identity I had ever
been taught that it was okay to have," Tim said. "But I just
never fit into that identity. I always felt like a failure for not
being masculine enough."

With the parable of the talents in mind, I asked Tim and

Sara what their church had taught about God when it came to sex and gender. I wanted to know: Were they the servant who'd buried his talent? And if so, what view of God had compelled them to do so?

"I saw God as a combination of creepy and easily disappointed," Tim responded. "I was told that God was always there to watch me masturbate and then make me feel bad about it. God would bless me sexually only as long as I followed the plan, and was disappointed in me if I didn't live up to certain 'man rules,' like being a spiritual leader and resisting temptation."

The church taught Tim and Sara that God was watching their every move, ready with a head shake. Like a controlling asshole with a killer surveillance system. And for a while that theology worked on Tim and Sara, as I know it has worked on so many. They buried their innate sexual development in order to please the master. And they entered marriage expecting their sex lives to be blessed accordingly.

Theology matters when we're talking about sexual stewardship. The parable of the talents shows us that our view of God will determine our view of what God has entrusted to us. Will it bring us flourishing and joy, or will it bring us fear and shame? How we view our creator defines how we view ourselves and others.*

I would argue that any theology that assumes God has placed humans like rats into a big lab experiment, giving us

---

* This has been shown in brain studies conducted by neuroscientist Andrew Newberg, MD. See Andrew Newberg and Mark Robert Waldman, *How God Changes Your Brain: Breakthrough Findings from a Leading Neuroscientist* (New York: Ballantine Books, 2009).

shocks for bad behavior and reward pellets for good behavior, is bad theology. So is any theology that assumes, even though God created humanity in mind-blowing diversity, that God is pleased only with a certain *type* of human.* This view of God has led so many of us to bury our sexual treasure out of fear. We deny our natures, identities, and desires in order to not anger an easily disappointed God. The result is suffering—outer darkness—and it's *not* of God's making.

But the plan that was handed to Tim and Sara—the plan that told them they must be celibate until marriage and then adhere to specific gender roles within their relationship in order for it to be healthy and pleasing to God—isn't actually a plan for pleasing God. In some ways, it's just a description of a particular type of person.

"My sister wasn't harmed at all by the same messages that set me up for failure," Tim said. "Following the plan worked for her. She is thriving in her marriage and otherwise."

But here's the thing much of the church has seemingly ignored: Tim's sister isn't thriving because she happens to be righteous. It's because she happens to naturally be the kind of person the plan describes—cis-gender, heterosexual, feminine, sweet, Christian, and a virgin when she got married. There's nothing wrong with any of that. But it doesn't make her special to God.

---

* Pastor and theologian Robert Capon speaks to this: "The church, by and large, has had a poor record of encouraging freedom. She has spent so much time inculcating in us the fear of making mistakes that she has made us like ill-taught piano students; we play our songs, but we never really hear them, because our main concern is not to make music, but to avoid some flub that will get us in dutch." *Between Noon and Three: Romance, Law, and the Outrage of Grace* (Grand Rapids, MI: Eerdmans, 1997), 148.

I think back to my conversation with Meghan on the edge of the stage. How there are people out there for whom everything the church taught *works*. People who *did* have fulfilling sex after a virgin engagement. People who *do* feel comfortable within the gender roles the church so often prescribes. Then I think of how Meghan touched her thumb and forefinger together and said, "Yeah, and this is how small that circle is." Even Tim and Sara—cis-gender, heterosexual, Christian, and married—don't fit in the circle of folks who've been watered and nourished by their church's teachings about sex. But that is not due to failure on their part; it is due to bad theology and its effects.

Like the way the rich guy in the parable knew that each of the three servants was different and thus gave them different talents, sexual stewardship means recognizing that every one of us has different wiring, different needs, different sins, different gifts, different sensitivities. It calls for *attention*.

To God, everyone is different but no one is *special*. You're not special for being straight. Or gay. Or male. Or cis. Or trans. Or asexual. Or married. Or sexually prodigious. Or a virgin. We all have the same God who placed the same image and likeness within us and entrusted us imperfect human beings with such mind-blowing things as sexuality and creativity and the ability as individuals to love and be loved as we are. The church may provide a center-pivot irrigation system for those in the small circle, but God provides *rain*. We don't earn rain, and we don't control it. We don't get to decide where it falls or in what amount. That shit is free.

.   .   .

Tim and Sara are figuring it out. When the church's plan failed them, it felt like outer darkness for a while, but they're starting to unearth the things they'd long ago buried. They've spent the last year in therapy alone and together, paying attention to who they really are as people. Tim is unashamed of not being a spiritual leader (whatever that means). Sara has figured out that she doesn't have to change or manipulate her husband; she can just love him for who he is. No more plan. One size *doesn't* fit all, and maybe it was never supposed to.

"Also," Sara added, "we aren't going to have kids. Before last year I never even considered that as an option, but once we let go of the plan, we realized having kids isn't something every young couple has to do or has to want."

They are becoming themselves, and truly seeing and loving each other, with all their quirks and beauty. God has given them gifts that are theirs and theirs alone, and they are learning to steward them in the best way that imperfect people can. And that is *good*.

"Wait," I said just as we were about to stand up to leave. "I have one more thing to talk about before we go. I know it may be a little weird." Sara and Tim looked at me curiously, maybe waiting for a pastoral admonition. Instead, I told them one of the reasons I decided to write this book. I want to tell you, too.

My husband of nearly twenty years and I didn't know how to connect. It wasn't his fault. He is a good man and a great father. But there was a part of me that was shut down for a very long time. It was hell for both of us, but finally we were able to face reality and walk with our family through an amicable separation and divorce.

When I started seeing my boyfriend, I felt connected to him and to my body and my desires and my erotic nature in a deep way. It was like an exfoliation of my entire spirit. It softened me and opened my heart and cleared away the gunk in my head. It was *good*. Not perfect. *Good*. Good like bodies. Good like chocolate cake. Good like when God saw what God made, and God looked at it and said it was good.

"Some clergy want to know if their congregants are giving money to the church," I continued. "They believe that stewardship can be a sign of spiritual health, that when we understand that everything we have is a gift from God, then we will be free and joyful about giving."

Tim and Sara shifted in the booth and looked at each other knowingly. This part sounded familiar to them.

"But," I added, "my experience, and your story, and the stories of so many of us at HFASS make me wonder: maybe a good sex life—whatever that looks like for who we are as individuals—can also be a sign of spiritual health. As your pastor, I want that part of your life and your relationship to be *good*. I want your sexual life to be free from fear and shame and to be joyful and true to who you are as individuals, because it is a holy gift from God."

They smiled and said, "We are getting there." And then we stood and hugged and said goodbye.

.   .   .

As I drove home, I thought about that time in my living room when we discussed our financial stewardship strategy. What we ultimately came to—besides the wish that we could actually make Stuart's T-shirts—was that we wouldn't have a stewardship plan. Instead, we would present our financial needs and hopes without any fanfare or emotionally manipulative teachings. If people wanted to give, they would give, according to their abilities.

So if you have been told that God is trying to trick you, if you have been told that your sexuality is good only if it is confined to a tiny circle, then you have been lied to, and I am so sorry. God gave you your gifts and never intended for them to be buried.

Whatever sexual flourishing looks like for you, that's what I would love to see happen in your life. Let us seek to be stewards of our bodies, to live in the joy of our createdness, honest about our shortcomings, soaking up the grace of God's rain. Let us find beauty and pleasure in our individual human bodies, trusting each other to use our gifts of sexuality according to our *dynamis*, our strength and capacity. Let us treat ourselves and others, no matter what our talents, as if we are all holy. Because we are.

HOOKED ON COLFAX

"When we told friends that we wanted to open a coffee shop on East Colfax, they warned us it was where the hookers hung out," Malissa, owner of Hooked on Colfax, recently recounted to me. "They said we'd get mugged. We decided to just embrace the bad reputation." She and her husband, Scott, wanted to create an inclusive, welcoming community space that featured locally roasted coffee and homemade treats. So in 2005 they opened Hooked on Colfax, the space from which I wrote much of this book. It sits on what *Playboy* once called "the longest, wickedest street in America."

Prostitution, drug dealing, and violence have dotted the twenty-five miles of Denver's gritty Colfax Avenue for decades.* In popular culture, both Jimmy from the animated TV show *South Park* and Jimmy from the film *Things to Do in Denver When You're Dead* have attempted to procure the services of prostitutes on this street. Sal Paradise from Jack Kerouac's Beat novel *On the Road* lives and drinks on Colfax.

On warm Denver days the garage door that doubles as the front wall of Hooked on Colfax opens up to the street, sharing the smells of espresso and freshly baked muffins with the cops and yogis and homeless folks walking down Colfax.

Inside, local art hangs above the open laptops of medical students and 1099 workers. A community bulletin board features fliers for protests, concerts, and tai chi classes, along with hand-drawn index cards. There's currently one advertising "Animal Guidance: finding your animal spirit(s) with guided meditation. $20 + location fees (general), $30 + location fees (shadow work). Ask me about my poverty/disability

---

* Denver Library's History of Colfax: https://history.denverlibrary.org/east-colfax-neighborhood.

discounts." I have no idea what any of that means, yet I find myself strangely comforted knowing that disabled folks who live in poverty can access shadow work animal spirit meditation for less than $30.

Hooked on Colfax is HFASS's church away from church: where we hold planning meetings and office hours and have pastoral care appointments. A perfect place to talk about faith and sex.

4

DOUBLE-STRANDED HELIX

One Saturday morning my parishioner Cindy and I sat in a booth at Hooked on Colfax as she told me her story.

"By the time I found myself sitting alone on my kitchen floor, surrounded by blood, a sharp knife next to me, my life had become one long game of spiritual Chutes and Ladders," she said. "I would try and try and climb and climb toward the goal of salvation, and then I would inevitably fail in some way and slide down again."

She looked up from her coffee, and I saw that Cindy's ice blue eyes matched her shirt almost exactly. Locks of short, graying hair curled around her face.

On that night twenty-two years ago in Seattle, as Cindy sat on the kitchen floor having just cut up her arms and legs, the sound of a phone call shook her back into consciousness. Her therapist, who had never called her at home before, just had a feeling that she should check in on Cindy.

"There's so much blood," Cindy told her wearily. "I

don't know what happened." The paramedics showed up soon afterward.

Despite her best efforts to climb her way up into God's favor, Cindy had felt as though she'd slid as far down as the chute could take her. And when she landed on the blood-soaked linoleum of her tiny apartment, it was as if the fractured pieces of herself had spilled all around her.

It had all started many years before, when she was sitting on a different floor. Cindy spent many weekends of her teenage years on church retreats designed to move young people toward sexual purity and "transcending their sinful bodies." And what better way to get kids to not think about sex than to send them to a cabin for a weekend with a team of adults who insisted they talk about nothing *but* sex? Sitting in a circle, being asked by the adult leaders how often they thought about sex, how they planned to stay pure, what the dangers of masturbation and homosexuality were, Cindy, regardless of what the truth was for her, began to feel pressure to come up with the right answers.

Cindy sincerely wanted to be close to God, to know God, and the leaders made clear to her exactly what that was supposed to look like. It certainly didn't look like the truth, which was that Cindy's desire was for her friend Marla. Thirteen-year-old Cindy may not have understood exactly what was going on with her body just yet. But she knew she liked Marla. A lot. Yet she also loved God.

So Cindy "split"; that's how she puts it. She cordoned off the parts of her that were "incompatible" with her desire to follow God and tried to forget about them. She became an avatar of herself, the version she was told God wanted her

to be. It was only later, after ten years of living a totally du-
plicitous life, that the consequences of being "split" caught
up with her.

In the Pentecostal church of Cindy's childhood, it was
made clear that there was one way to be close to God:
to seek God with everything you had. Among other things,
seeking God was accomplished by being slain in the Spirit,
undergoing exorcisms, and speaking in tongues.

Cindy *wanted* to want these things. She wanted to want
the gift of speaking in tongues like Quaker kids want to
want simplicity and hippie kids want to want to be mellow.

But the exorcisms were terrifying for Cindy. Demons
were believed to have taken over the bodies of those who
"struggled with homosexuality" or who did not adhere to
the church's small circle of acceptability. If you suffered
chronic illness, or struggled with a tiny bit of sleeping with
your secretary, or just happened to like the music of Led
Zeppelin (which was considered demonic at the time), the
church would subject you to a violent religious ritual. A
group of men surrounded you at the front of church, right
in the middle of the service, and demanded that your demon
come out.

"Come out, demon! Release this boy!" the men would shout.
*"In the name of Jesus I command you to leave this body! You have
no authority here!"*

The men yelled, sometimes with absolute conviction and
other times in desperate pleading. Cindy never knew if the
men shouted because they were worried it wouldn't work

or maybe because demons were hard of hearing. Sometimes during an exorcism, the pastor would ask the demon to name itself. And the person might yell back, in a weird mechanical voice, something like *"I am the demon of masturbation!"* (Not surprisingly, there were lots of sex-related exorcisms in Cindy's church.) From behind the protective cascade of her long curly hair, Cindy would watch as the boy with the Led Zeppelin demon or the man with the demon of masturbation shouted and grunted and made guttural sounds. They thrashed violently around on the floor—sweating, writhing, sometimes vomiting—before releasing into a state of surrender and peace.

Cindy watched all of this with a mix of conflicting emotions and confusing questions: Why did they have to do this? The people seemed okay to her. Could a demon just slip into *her* without her knowing it? Had one already? Was that why she had feelings for Marla?

Part of her wanted to go up there, wanted to feel calm and free from the struggle she experienced in her body. But the fear of becoming a religious spectacle was stronger, so when she sensed the preacher looking her way, she pretended to read her Bible, which she'd kept open on her lap. A demon wouldn't read the Bible, would it?

"We were being told to be vigilant with our bodies," Cindy said to me as Bob Dylan played over the speakers. But as high school progressed, this project of vigilance got harder and harder for Cindy.

We'd been at Hooked for an hour, past the midmorning rush, where you can barely hear the music over the din. Now, in the quieter space, Dylan's folksy whine—*how many years can some people exist / before they're allowed to be free?*—punctuated our conversation.

During sophomore year, Marla started leading some of the weekend retreat conversations. Everything seemed so easy for her, Cindy thought. Her petite, shiny-haired friend spoke in tongues and talked with ease about the dangers of masturbation and passed tissues to the kids who inevitably started crying. Marla seemed so happy, so close to God, so Christian. Cindy would have followed her anywhere. At night, after the prayer meeting, after the kids had dried their tears and the ones who had vomited were cared for and cleaned up, the two adult leaders would disappear (she learned later they were having an affair), and Marla would encourage Cindy to walk outside with her. "Under the stars, in God's creation, it is going to be easier for you to find your prayer language," she said to Cindy one night. Cindy nodded and reached out for a hug.

Back at home, Marla and Cindy would spend hours huddled together in Marla's "prayer closet," perched on a yellow-flowered pillow that left barely enough room for the two girls. At one end of the closet sat a small altar, which Marla had lit with a tiny flashlight.

"There we would sit," Cindy said, "a couple of fourteen-year-old girls, praying that I might speak in tongues. My arm entwined with Marla's, we would plead with the Almighty to help me climb another rung of the holiness ladder."

The emotion and intimacy of the time in the prayer closet might not have brought Cindy closer to actually speaking in tongues, but it did bring her closer to Marla. So Cindy started to *pretend* she could speak in tongues. She'd heard the cadence and sound of it enough in her life that she could mimic it convincingly. Still, she thought so much about being close to Marla that in her earnest mind, she believed that any progress up that ladder was lost. Down the chute she'd tumble.

By the time she left for college, the church's pastor had confessed to an affair with the choir director. He stood in front of his congregation, in the very spot from which he'd preached sermons on sexual purity, and was himself exorcised of the demon of sexual impurity. "If the devil is powerful enough to tempt even your pastor," he said before the ritual, "then he is powerful indeed."

Cindy attended an Evangelical college in the Pacific Northwest, where she lied about her Pentecostal upbringing, embarrassed as she was about the fainting and casting out of demons. Her senior year, she began having an affair with the pastor's wife, a relationship that lasted two years, all while she was also engaged to the lead singer of the college's praise band.

After college, Cindy kept up the act. She married her worship-leader boyfriend and began to teach high school. At night she'd alternate between sneaking off with her lover one evening and going to church events the next. She tried to both transcend her body and listen to it, and the conflict between the two undid her. When her marriage unsurprisingly ended after just ten months, she unraveled further. The real parts of herself and the made-up stories blurred into confusion, until that one evening when Cindy, sprawled out bleeding on the kitchen floor, was saved by a phone call from her therapist.

"It wasn't a suicide attempt," Cindy told me at the coffee shop that day. "It wasn't even a 'cry for help,' as they say. I cut my arms and legs that night without even realizing what was happening. I think I was desperate to feel something real, something I *wasn't* faking."

Cindy stayed in a psych unit for two weeks, where she finally stopped pretending. She told the doctors and other patients her story about her split life and her spiritual chutes and ladders. When she did, she felt things in her body that she'd become so unfamiliar with. Simple human things, like hunger for food and the need for sleep. It was the beginning of her reassembly. Like a double-stranded helix, she came back together one molecule at a time.

In ancient Greek, the root of *demon* means "to throw apart."* That which causes us to fracture, to become less whole, is demonic.

In Mark's Gospel, Jesus casts out a demon from a young man who, "night and day among the tombs . . . would cry out and cut himself." But first Jesus asked the demon to name itself (Mark 5:5–9). When I read this story, I think of

---

* From Dictionary.com: "From Greek *daimon*, 'deity, divine power; lesser god; guiding spirit, tutelary deity' (sometimes including souls of the dead); 'one's genius, lot, or fortune'; from PIE *dai-mon-* 'divider, provider' (of fortunes or destinies), from root *da-* 'to divide.'"

Cindy sitting on the floor of that crappy apartment, crying out, cutting her arms and legs so that she could finally just feel something. If this is what having a demon is, then what name shall we give hers? Let's call hers shame. Shame slid its way into her body and divided her from herself. It separated her earnest pursuit of God from her body, from her mind, from her sexuality, from her heart.

I like to think that when Jesus sent the disciples to cast out demons in his name, he intended for them to look with so much love upon those who had become fractured that their neglected pieces returned to the center of their being. He intended that the parts that were deemed unlovable by somebody or some institution—the parts abused by those who were supposed to love and protect them—could, in the gaze of such love, reassemble.

Cindy found healing, but at first it was outside of Christianity—at a Lakota sweat lodge in Wyoming. Gathered with a dozen women in the extreme darkness and heat, she prayed to God without doctrine, without judgment, without the distraction of having to be or say or believe anything in particular. There was nothing to pretend.

She sat in a circle with others again, like at the youth retreats. But here she sweated away the shame that no longer served her. There was no ladder of virtue, no chute of vice. There was only the heat from the stones on her skin, the smell of the sage in her nostrils, the sound of the chanted prayer in her ears, and the darkness of the lodge in her eyes.

There at the sweat lodge, she told me, her double helix

reattached, knitting back together the physical, spiritual, sexual, and emotional parts of herself. There was no longer a sinful body to transcend. There was just her, all of her, coming together, united in holiness—cell by cell, prayer by prayer, drop of sweat by drop of sweat.

One weekend, Cindy arrived early so she could burn something in the fire. She stood outside the lodge with a couple of close friends by her side, their faces focused on the flames before them, the stones for the lodge glowing red under the burning wood. In a few minutes, those stones would be carried into the lodge, and pinches of sweetgrass and cedar would be tossed on top, the cleansing incense of purification releasing in the air before the doors closed. But for now the stones rested under the wood of the fire pit, ready to receive that which needed to burn.

Cindy reached into her bag and took out her Bible, the same Bible that had sat in her lap in that cabin as a teenage girl, the one she had pretended to read to avoid exorcism, the one in whose margins she had scribbled desperate notes, like a book of spells by which she could transfigure herself.

Slowly, without words, she tore out eight very specific pages from her Bible—namely, those that mentioned homosexuality—and burned them one by one. As she stood there watching the inferno, she felt as if the people of her childhood church, the youth workers and pastors and other adults, rose from the grave of her psyche and stood in judgment of her around that fire. She saw them, but she didn't care. She was allowing herself to be free.

But she wasn't quite done.

Cindy then tore out the Gospels: Matthew, Mark, Luke,

John. The story of Jesus had never hurt her; Jesus had never asked her to split. So with her right hand she clutched the pages of the Gospels over her heart, and with her left she tossed in the rest to burn.

There are those who will say that it is "dangerous" to think we can decide for ourselves what is sacred in the Bible and what is not. I reject this idea, and here's why. The Gospels are the canon within the canon. The Bible, as Martin Luther said, is the cradle that holds Christ. The point of gravity is the story of Jesus, the Gospel. The closer a text of the Bible is to that story or to the heart of that story's message, the more authority it has. The farther away it is, the less its authority.

It's a story of how the God who spoke through prophets and poets was the same God who showed up later in a human body and walked around like he didn't understand the rules. Jesus said God's world is like a father running into the road to meet his no-good child as if the child's no-goodness was no matter.

Jesus' stories seemed like nonsense, but then they also seemed like absolute truth at the same time. He just kept saying that the things we think are so important rarely are: things like holding grudges and making judgments and hoarding wealth and being first. Then one night, this Jesus got all weird at dinner and said a loaf of bread was his body and a cup of wine was his blood, and all of it is for forgiveness. All of it means our no-goodness is no matter. Then he went and got himself killed in a totally preventable way. Three days later he blew his friends' minds by showing back up and being all like, "You guys have any snacks? I'm starving." Then he made a fire, grilled some fish, and invited his friends to join him. It is this same Jesus that stood by Cindy as she freed herself around a sweat lodge fire, clutching his story to her breast.

The first Saturday in December, six months after hearing Cindy's story, I made my way up the wooden steps of a renovated barn outside of Denver. The Great Advent Gospel Read-Aloud is a yearly tradition for House for All Sinners and Saints, a day when we gather around in a big circle of sofas and chairs, a hearty table of snacks nearby, knitting or other crafts in hand, and read the Gospels out loud chapter by chapter, everyone taking a turn.

Cindy sat at a table close by, still in the circle of furniture, drawing on a piece of watercolor paper.

Travis, our resident Korean American electrician and judo instructor, was reading from Mark 5 about the man from whom Jesus cast out an entire legion of demons, demons that had tormented the man, body and soul.

"Then people came out to see what had happened," Travis said, "and when they came to Jesus, they found the man from whom the demons had gone sitting at the feet of Jesus, clothed and in his right mind."

I looked at Cindy. She, too, was sitting at the feet of Jesus, the one who had never hurt her, clothed and in her right mind. She caught my eye, smiled, and lifted up the text from which she was following along.

"No way!" I mouthed, my eyes wide.

In Cindy's hands were the Gospels from her childhood

Bible—Matthew, Mark, Luke, and John—which she had clutched to her heart that evening twenty years ago at the lodge. She'd fashioned a binding for the pages out of a braided cord of sweetgrass and kept them all these years.

That night at the lodge, there had been a full moon, the image of which Cindy had since rendered in watercolor over Matthew's opening story about Jesus' genealogy and infancy. Layers of soft gray cover the page, depicting the night sky, with the words "never again" painted across the top. Then, down among the rows of text, an image of a full moon, a small white orb of light among the darkness, surrounds a single word: "Jesus."

Courtesy of Cindy. Used with permission.

THEY BELONGED TO EACH OTHER

ON THE DAY God created the heavens and the earth, there weren't any plants yet because there wasn't any water yet because there wasn't anyone to do the gardening yet. God didn't rush. Shit has to happen in a certain order for this to work.

Then God formed an earthling (Adam is a genderless word for "from the earth") out of dirt, and God breathed into the earthling's nose to animate us, and this is how we received a soul and the gift of life.

We are dirt and the breath of God.

Then God put on some overalls, grabbed a pitchfork, and planted the most amazing garden in Eden, then put the earthling in the garden God had made for us. God made some really beautiful trees that not only were pleasurable to look at but also made the most delicious fruit for us to eat. And there were two special trees in the garden: the tree of life (the knowledge of God) and the tree of knowledge of good and evil.

God is more of a starter than a maintainer. More entrepreneur than manager. So God gave the garden to the earthling to care for, because God's got other things to do. And God was like, "I hooked you up with some really killer fruit trees, so enjoy them! That's living. But don't eat from that one tree. Let me worry about the what-is-good-and-evil stuff. I don't want this to become about that for you. I want you to just live. I'll be the creator, and you'll be the creature."

Then God thought about what it felt like to be alone and realized that it would kind of suck for the earthling to do all this living and fruit-eating and gardening with no one else around. So out of the dirt God created every animal of the field and bird of the air, and then God entertained God's self by seeing what the earthling would name these birds and beasts. And they were cool, but none of them was a partner. I mean, chickens are awesome, but they can't plow for shit.

So God thought, "Maybe trying to make more creatures from dirt isn't doing the trick. I should make one out of flesh." So God snuck up behind the earthling with a chloroform-soaked handkerchief and made the earthling "sleep," and then for some reason God took a rib out of the earthling and sewed the earthling back up and made a female. And then God gave the two earthlings to each other because they belonged that way. They were made for and from each other. And they fit. And this is why still to this day, many of us need to fit with someone else, emotionally, sexually, and spiritually.

And the two earthlings, male and female, were naked. And they were not ashamed. Shame hadn't been introduced yet. That comes soon enough.

5

HOLY RESISTANCE

WE AFFIRM that self-conception as male or female
should be defined by God's holy purposes in creation and redemption as revealed in Scripture.

WE DENY that adopting a homosexual or transgender
self-conception is consistent with God's holy purposes in creation and redemption.

—The Nashville Statement, article 7

Here is a loose timeline of what I did the week the city
of Houston was under the waters of Hurricane Harvey, the
week when the forty-fifth president of the United States
announced he would end a federal program that protected
undocumented immigrant children, and the week when
a Southern Baptist organization published the Nashville
Statement, a document that outlines all of the reasons being
gay or transgender is outside of God's "plan for humanity."

Sunday: My son, Judah, and I said goodbye to my only

daughter, his sister, as she left for a small women's college in Oakland. I was filled with grief, and also excitement. But mostly grief. She was my heart. My friend.

I know, I know, you're not supposed to be "friends" with your kids. You're supposed to be a parent. The giver of tough love. The buck-stopping authority who lays down the law. But after years of butting heads and competing over who was more willful, the time in which Harper needed any of that had passed. We slowly just kind of moved into being two women who liked each other and enjoyed spending time in each other's company. And yet, still, she was my baby, the one who made me a mom, the one who grew in my womb, nursed at my breast in my mother's antique rocking chair, and became a person in front of my eyes. My baby. My heart. And I had to stand next to her brother in my ex-husband's driveway and wave as he and our baby left for California.

I said a million prayers that day. "Protect her, God. Send her friends who see how amazing she is. Help her remember to get all her homework done before she parties." Those would have to be enough. I hugged Judah a bit too tightly and then we made breakfast.

Tuesday: After the gym, I tried to write about gender norms but got stuck when I read this insane quote from William W. Orr, a pastor who published a Christian sex-ed book in the 1950s. Partly because it just sounded gay as hell:

> Adam was masculine, strong, capable. He must have been a handsome spectacle as he stood there, clean, fresh, pure from the hand of God. Possibly six feet tall, muscular body, square shoulders, deep chest, prominent chin, with

perhaps a dimple in it. Every inch a man's man. Eve must have loved him so much it hurt.

And Eve. What a vision of perfect delight she must have been. Her skin soft and lovely, her hair long and silky. I'm sure her form was feminine to the core. She must have had delicately formed hands and dainty feet. Her eyes were blue as the skies above, and her lips shamed the redness of the rose. Surely, the admiration of her husband must have been nearly worship.

Here's the beginning of God's sex plan. Manly men and womanly women.*

Having given in to distraction already, I posted this quote in my congregation's Facebook group, along with a snarky comment about how white this Adam and Eve sounded, with the blue eyes and silky hair and whatnot. Almost immediately, one of my parishioners noted, "This doesn't sound much different from the Nashville Statement." "Totally!" another person replied.

I didn't know what they were talking about, so even though I was about to leave for coffee with my parishioner Kevin and didn't have the time to get pulled into internet drama, I asked for a link, because I am also a sucker.

The Nashville Statement, written by a group whose name I could not possibly make up—the Center for Biblical Manhood and Womanhood—and signed by big-name pastors from a bunch of influential churches, is a document that

---

* William W. Orr, *Plain Talk About Love and Sex* (Wheaton, IL: Scripture Press, 1950).

doubles down on conservative Christian views on sexuality and gender. The preamble states, "We are not our own. Our true identity, as male and female persons, is given by God. It is not only foolish, but hopeless, to try to make ourselves what God did not create us to be."

I sat in my apartment and read the fourteen articles of the Nashville Statement, each punching me anew in the stomach, one after another. I had just spent months interviewing dozens of my parishioners for this book, asking each of them three questions: (1) Growing up, what messages did you receive from church about sex and the body? (2) How did these messages affect you? (3) How have you navigated your life now as an adult?

Parishioner after parishioner recounted horrible things that were said and done to them in Christian settings. The woman who believed for twenty years that God never gave her a husband because she'd had an abortion when she was sixteen. The gay man who was forced into a "reparative" program designed to make him an ex-gay man, where a male therapist coerced him into sex. The trans folk who self-harmed, cutting into their own skin because they didn't know they could instead cut into the utter bullshit the church fed them about existing outside of God's ordained gender roles.

I wish so much that I could sit down with the people who wrote the Nashville Statement and tell them the stories I have heard from these faithful people God loves. I wish I could show them how their loyalty to a doctrine or an interpretation of a few Bible verses has created harm in the bodies and spirits of the people in my care. It may be comforting to believe God has some kind of master blueprint for gender expression and sexual relationships, which if followed correctly will allow us all to build happy, fulfilled lives, and that veering from that plan is dangerous. I see the appeal of that as an *idea*. But I want to remind the drafters of the Nashville Statement that when people asked Jesus how to be righteous and live in God's plan and be pleasing to the Lord, Jesus didn't say "Don't be trans" or "Don't have sex outside of marriage." He just said, "Love God, and love your neighbor as yourself" (Mark 12:30–31).

Loving your neighbor sounds nice, even easy. But unfortunately it means I should show concern not just for the nice lady who lives next door but also for the Center for Biblical Manhood and Womanhood—my neighbors of last resort, the ones I'd prefer to not love at all.

I know that as women speak up and claim our dignity, as queer folks speak up and claim theirs, and as our society increasingly embraces the wild diversity within the human race, it's not easy to resist it all. The drafters of the Nashville Statement admit as much in their preamble: "Evangelical Christians at the dawn of the twenty-first century find themselves living in a period of historic transition. As Western culture has become increasingly post-Christian, it has embarked upon a massive revision of what it means to be a human being." They are losing the culture war, and that can't feel good. This tiny little morsel of compassion is all I can manage.

I looked at the clock, closed my laptop, and texted Kevin that I was going to be about seven minutes late.

.   .   .

Kevin works in investment banking, but he looks like a farm boy with his trim blond beard and Carhartt shirt. He's twenty-five years old, "masculine, strong, capable, every inch a man's man," as William Orr may have described him. He also happens to be transgender. "But I pass," he admitted. "Like, no one knows unless I tell them."

Kevin told me about being raised in the Midwest in a loving family that didn't seem terribly bothered by religion, and I thought about how lucky he was to have come to the Christian faith as an adult. Coming out as trans is hard enough for anyone, but unlike most of his queer compatriots at church, Kevin didn't have a family that fed him spoonfuls of self-hatred and told him it was "God's plan" for his life.

A few weeks prior to our meeting, Kevin was baptized at House for All Sinners and Saints. "I just find the idea of forgiveness something that is really needed, and where I find it is in the story of Jesus. I need that story. I want in," he said. Still fuming over the Nashville Statement, I was slightly irritated to be reminded of Jesus' message by a new Christian when what I rather would've done was rant about the shit that was making me hate people.

Looking at this sweet-natured, farm-boy-looking young man across from me, I just couldn't understand why the religious types of our day see him as a threat, or why the lawmakers and voters of North Carolina would prefer that he use the women's restroom. Why would the drafters of the Nashville Statement want him to believe that by his very nature, he goes against the will of God?

The transgender thing can be hard for people my age and older. I get that. I'm nearly fifty, and it's taken me a while to catch up. Even with as many trans and gender-queer people as I have in my life, I still don't always under-stand. And then I remember: it doesn't matter. The fact that I sometimes don't get it is *my* shit, and I should not confuse my shit with my job. My job is to just love my parishioners. And I do. Not perfectly, but I do.

Kevin and I said goodbye, and I walked downstairs to the speakeasy beneath Hooked on Colfax. Between reading the Nashville Statement that morning and leaving for coffee with Kevin, I'd quickly popped back onto my congrega-tion's Facebook group and invited whoever was interested to join me at the coffee shop for a tiny bit of "editing work." Half a dozen of my parishioners were already sitting at a table, hunched over their laptops.

As my eyes adjusted to the dim light, I saw Meghan, the middle-aged transwoman who taught me about small circles, and who completes the *New York Times* crossword puzzle every day of her life; Cody, a young gay man who was new at church and yet seems to show up to every pot-luck with a massive amount of homemade comfort food; Whitney and Jenny, who are engaged to be married and who met while friends at Calvin College, a conservative Christian school; and Lori and her nineteen-year-old queer daughter, Miriam.

Together, we spent the afternoon drafting what we called the Denver Statement, a line-by-line rewriting of the Nashville Statement. We started with the preamble:

Christians at the dawn of the twenty-first century find
themselves living in an exciting, beautiful, liberating,

and holy period of historic transition. Western culture has embarked upon a massive revision of what it means to be a human being by expanding the limits and definitions previously imposed by the church. By and large, the spirit of our age discerns and delights in the beauty of God's design for human life that is so much richer and more diverse than we have previously understood it to be.

We sat around a table in the corner of the cafe basement, eating scones, drinking coffee, and reading each article, one by one, and collectively offering edits. It felt like liturgy. We'd gathered together to honor one another's voices and personhood, and we listened for God amidst those voices. We laughed, teared up, noticed and gave grace.

Hours later, when we finally finished, Cody said, "This was better than therapy."

Several of us then drove the two miles west down Colfax, past crowded bus stops, pizza parlors, and porn shops, and then north half a block to the church for our first-ever music salon. Since our worship services at House have no musical instruments, no band, no organ, nothing but human voices, some of the musician types had decided to host an event where people could showcase their other talents. To be honest, I was kind of dreading it. I pictured the whole thing turning awkward when someone inevitably got up to sing "You Light Up My Life" to a prerecorded background track. (You know, like I may or may not have done at a Christian summer camp when I was twelve.)

But the music salon wasn't awkward. It was glorious. Classical pieces played by people who I'd had no idea pos-

sessed that insane level of talent, soul-churning perfor-
mances from singer-songwriters, and a particularly moving
cello arrangement. But what killed me was Winnie, a curvy
Ugandan woman who, with a giant smile and even bigger
energy, sang a rendition of a song from *The Little Mermaid*,
but with lyrics of her own:

Part of Your Citizenship

(To the tune of The Little Mermaid*'s "Part of Your World")*

Look at this country, isn't it neat
Wouldn't you think immigration is sweet
Wouldn't you think I'm the girl
The girl who wants just one thing
I wanna be
Where the Americans are
I want to vote
Since millennials are lame
Someday I'll have money to pay for (wait, what's it called?)
Oh, health insurance
Usually in a week I can get by
Selling my kidney wasn't so bad
Wish I could be
Part of your citizenship

As I sat along the wall listening to this beautiful woman
(who to many is not a beautiful young woman but an "illegal immigrant"), I wondered why people like Kevin and
Winnie so often get cast as "issues" by people who don't
know a single thing about them. All of this, as I sat with

my laptop and finished formatting our draft of the Denver Statement.

When I looked up, I saw that Cody—the potluck prince—had taken a seat right next to me. I grabbed his hand, and together we hit "publish."

Wednesday: I allowed myself to read exactly six negative Facebook comments in response to the Denver Statement. Most of them accused me and my congregation of "not believing God's Word" or not adhering to the authority of scripture. But I couldn't dwell on these accusations for long, because I needed to do what I do most weeks of my life—which is to read and study the Bible, the very thing I was accused of ignoring.

Preaching at House for All Sinners and Saints involves a great deal of time spent obsessing over whatever scriptural text happens to be assigned for that Sunday. All week I think about the text in the shower, while I walk my dog, and while I am driving. After meeting people for pastoral care, I often ask if they can read the text with me and tell me what stands out to them. When I awaken in the middle of the night, I've trained my brain not to jump to my to-do list or whatever is bothering me at the moment, but instead to start thinking through the week's Bible text until I fall back asleep. Being a preacher is like having a not-very-interesting mental illness.

But I have found that if meditated on, wrestled with, and questioned properly, the Bible hands over the goods.

Not a blueprint, plan, or ultimatum, but a story of God and God's people that endures from generation to generation.

This week's text was from Exodus, one of only six books in the Bible that pass the Bechdel test, which requires that at some point in a piece of film or literature, two female characters must have a conversation with each other about something other than a man.* That's it. A low bar, certainly, yet it's seldom met.

The Exodus reading was a story of holy resistance. A story of how five defiant young women led the way to freedom for the Hebrew people. It goes like this: For several generations, the Israelites had lived peaceably in Egypt as resident aliens, but there was a new pharaoh, and he was a piece of work. He was, how shall I put this . . . an insecure, tyrannical racist who was lacking in wisdom. It happens.

Throughout history, recent and ancient, insecure leaders like to cast those with less power as "dangerous." Like when immigrants (such as my parishioner Winnie) are held responsible for a decline in the job market, or gay people (such as Cody) are deemed responsible for the divorce rate (having weakened the institution of marriage—as if straight people didn't take care of that already), and how it goes without saying that trans people (like my parishioner Emery, a lieutenant in the Army Signal Corps) are the reason the U.S. military costs so much money.

Pharaoh was no different. He looked around and said,

---

* The test is named for Alison Bechdel, the lesbian cartoonist and writer who came up with it. The six books of the Bible that pass the test are Exodus, Ruth, Samuel, Kings, Mark, and Luke.

"Hey, those Hebrew people sure do have a lot of babies. If that keeps up, this land will be filled with people who speak a different language and have a different skin color than the people who actually belong here." So Pharaoh came up with a solution to get rid of his "Hebrew issue." He started by enslaving them with forced labor, but that didn't work. They kept having babies. (Maybe because when life got so harsh and there were so few pleasures to be had, sex was one thing Pharaoh couldn't take from them.) So Pharaoh found a couple of midwives, Puah and Shiphrah, and told them to deal with the "Hebrew issue" by killing any newborn Hebrew boys. Girls, on the other hand, would be allowed to live. (Because what threat could girls pose?)

But Pharaoh underestimated the power of pissed-off women who want to protect the weak and guard the innocent—which perhaps is what it means when the text says "the midwives feared God." They respected God, they trusted God, they loved God, and they knew the difference between Pharaoh and God. Fear in this sense isn't terror. It's reverence. The fear Pharaoh felt, on the other hand—that's just *fear* fear. Fear of losing your importance or power or standing. Fear of the culture around you changing. This is not reverence, it's smallness, and it motivates things like decrees and statements about slaves and immigrants and queers.

Shiphrah and Puah were filled with the Holy Spirit and given the bravery and love to defy Pharaoh, and that's exactly what they did. They disobeyed him. They let the baby boys live. Because sometimes the most holy thing we can say is: *No. Not on my watch.*

When Pharaoh summoned the midwives again to ask

why they had disobeyed his order to take care of the "Hebrew issue," Shiphrah and Puah wisely answered the king by playing into his racist stereotypes. "Oh yeah," they said, "we totally want to kill all the boy babies, except those Hebrew women are not at all like your little Egyptian women. They are sturdy as hell—maybe it was all that slavery—and they can give birth like nobody's business. By the time we got over to their slave quarters, it was too late. They'd given birth already."

Pharaoh was stunned. Slavery hadn't solved his "Hebrew problem," and trying to manipulate midwives didn't solve it, either. So the next thing he tried was signing an executive order that decreed *all* Egyptians must look for baby boys born to Hebrew women and throw them in the Nile.

At this point, the story shifts to a young Hebrew woman who'd been hiding her beautiful boy baby from Pharaoh for as long as she could. After three months, though, her son grew too large to hide, and she was forced to do the unimaginable. She got a basket, plastered it with bitumen and pitch and what I can only imagine were a million prayers, then nestled the child in it and placed the basket among the reeds on the bank of the river. "Protect him, God," she prayed. That would have to be enough.

Not much later, Pharaoh's daughter came down to bathe at the river and saw the basket among the reeds. Curious, she looked in that basket and saw the child: his tiny arms, his perfect mouth, his little chest rising and falling with the breath of life, and she decided, *This is not an issue. It's a* baby.

She, too, was filled with God's spirit. Pharaoh's own daughter defied him by seeing the baby as a baby and not as an immigrant issue or a Hebrew issue—or a queer issue, or a woman issue, or a special-needs-population issue, or a black issue.

Then the baby's big sister, who'd apparently been monitoring the situation, stepped out from behind the reeds and did something so smart and loyal and loving and scheming that I will admire her all the days of my life. She said to Pharaoh's daughter, "Hey, I know a Hebrew woman who could totally be his wet nurse!" Pharaoh's daughter agreed, and the girl went home.

"He's alive, Mama," I imagine the sister saying with a catch in her voice that gave way to something fiercer. "And guess what—Pharaoh's daughter is literally going to pay you to breastfeed your baby boy. *With Pharaoh's own money!*"

Later, after the mother had weaned the child, she brought him to Pharaoh's daughter, who took him as her son. She named him Moses, which means "I drew him out of the water."

That was the text I would preach on Sunday.

Sunday: I know a lot about only a couple of things in this world, and one of those things is my congregation at House for All Sinners and Saints. In many ways they are a group of people who have made their own rafts sealed with pitch and prayer. As if together they have floated away from those who would do them harm, and somehow ended up back at church.

I've been invited into their stories. Their hearts and hurts and bodies and concerns and beauty have changed me.

So when a statement is made or an executive order is passed in which they are referred to as an "issue" or a "sin," I take that shit personally.

Maybe you do, too.

I can't imagine working through the kind of anger and sadness I felt that week, let alone preaching about it, without scripture. I didn't know what to do or say—all I could do was offer them this story of defiant young women who did the holy thing of saying "No, not on our watch." How could I survive without scripture? Lord, to whom shall we go? *You* have the words of eternal life.

When Sunday came, after a week filled with so much horrific news, I stood before my congregation and spoke with a voice shaking with love. "You are not an 'issue,'" I said, almost pleading for them to hear me. "You are not a mistake. You are not anything but what your God has created you to be. I will stand by you. We will stand by each other. And there is a source for all the love we need, a source for all the bravery we need. There is a source for all the defiance we need, and that source is not our ability to be right about everything; it is not the purity of our politics. The source of our defiance comes from the very same source that five young women in Egypt drew upon as they fought for freedom. That source is the God of Shiphrah and Puah."

And one more thing: Underestimate girls and trans folks and immigrants at your peril. We are totally a threat. God has sprinkled midwives and Pharaoh's daughters and other holy people all over the place whose job is to birth life from death.

DENVER VS. NASHVILLE

(NASHVILLE) WE AFFIRM that God's revealed will for all people is chastity outside of marriage and fidelity within marriage.

WE DENY that any affections, desires, or commitments ever justify sexual intercourse before or outside marriage; nor do they justify any form of sexual immorality.

(DENVER) **WE AFFIRM that God created us as sexual beings in endless variety.**

WE DENY that the only type of sexual expression that can be considered holy is between a cis-gender, heterosexual, married couple who waited to have sex until they were married. But if you fit in that group, good for you, we have no problem with your lifestyle choices.

(NASHVILLE) WE AFFIRM that God created Adam and Eve, the first human beings, in his own image, equal before God as persons, and distinct as male and female.

WE DENY that the divinely ordained differences between male and female render them unequal in dignity or worth.

(DENVER) **WE AFFIRM that God created Adam and Eve, the first human beings, in God's male and female image, and that all human beings share this image of God in common but express it differently in body and spirit.**

WE DENY that we as human beings can fully conceive of the glory of God's image or rightfully believe our language can define its limits. Therefore, we deny that those who do not conform to society's gender norms are outside of some kind of "divine plan."

(NASHVILLE) WE AFFIRM that self-conception as male or female should be defined by God's holy purposes in creation and redemption as revealed in Scripture.

WE DENY that adopting a homosexual or transgender self-conception is consistent with God's holy purposes in creation and redemption.

(DENVER) **WE AFFIRM that there is no longer male or female but all are one in Christ Jesus our Lord.**

WE DENY any self-conception that presumes one is capable of knowing God's holy purposes for other people, and that such self-conceptions can be consistent with the Gospel of grace, love, and mercy as demonstrated in holy scripture.

(NASHVILLE) WE AFFIRM that sin distorts sexual desires by directing them away from the marriage covenant and toward sexual immorality—a distortion that includes both heterosexual and homosexual immorality.

WE DENY that an enduring pattern of desire for sexual immorality justifies sexually immoral behavior.

(DENVER) **WE AFFIRM that sin distorts all aspects of human life.**

WE DENY that human beings can escape sin by simply upholding a particular doctrine or lifestyle.

(NASHVILLE) WE AFFIRM that it is sinful to approve of homosexual immorality or transgenderism and that such approval constitutes an essential departure from Christian faithfulness and witness.

WE DENY that the approval of homosexual immorality or trans-genderism is a matter of moral indifference about which other-wise faithful Christians should agree to disagree.

(DENVER) **WE AFFIRM that it is for freedom that Christ has set us free, and while we believe in the full inclusion of all people into the body of Christ (here we stand; we can do no other), we cannot bind the conscience of other Christians.**

WE DENY that it is sinful to approve of queer identities and that such approval constitutes an essential departure from Christian faithfulness and witness.

(NASHVILLE) WE AFFIRM that the grace of God in Christ enables sinners to forsake transgender self-conceptions and by divine forbearance to accept the God-ordained link between one's biological sex and one's self-conception as male or female.

WE DENY that the grace of God in Christ sanctions self-conceptions that are at odds with God's revealed will.

(DENVER) **WE AFFIRM that the grace of God in Christ enables sinners to forsake prejudice and see such prejudice as our own and not as God's.**

WE DENY that the grace of God in Christ sanctions self-righteous assertions of absolute knowledge of God's will.

(NASHVILLE) WE AFFIRM that Christ Jesus has come into the world to save sinners and that through Christ's death and resurrection forgiveness of sins and eternal life are available to every person who repents of sin and trusts in Christ alone as Savior, Lord, and supreme treasure.

WE DENY that the Lord's arm is too short to save or that any sinner is beyond his reach.

(DENVER) **WE AFFIRM that Christ Jesus has come into the world to save sinners and that through Christ's death and resurrection forgiveness of sins and eternal life are available to every person; this is a supreme treasure.**

WE DENY that God is a boy and has actual arms.★

★ There were fourteen articles in all, and after an hour and a half of work, we were . . . weary.

6

THE ROCKING CHAIR

I think we know that prior to the Lord putting
breath of life into Adam he had a heart, he had a
brain with vessels, and these vessels and heart were
filled with blood just as the vessels and heart of a
fetus are filled with blood. However, Adam did not
become a living soul until after the Lord breathed
into him the breath of life.

—Robert L. Pettus Jr., MD, *As I See Sex
Through the Bible*, 1973

"If you prefer crunchy peanut butter, cross the room," one
of my fellow camp counselors said.

A group of about sixty preteens sorted themselves into
groups by walking across the worn, wooden floors of the
summer camp rec hall. They giggled and intentionally
bumped into each other. A lanky red-haired boy gave a
high five to a mixed-race kid in a baseball cap. "Hell yeah,
creamy sucks," he said.

As soon as the students settled at their destinations, the counselor asked another question. "If you ever played hooky, cross the room." The students giggled and sorted themselves again. The hooky-playing kids included the ones you would've guessed, but also some surprises. No one had expected that Jessica had it in her. But that's what made this activity great.

From there, the questions got more vulnerable. "If your parents are divorced, cross the room." The high fives stopped as a couple of dozen kids headed to the far wall.

In the smaller groupings that formed as the activity progressed—the ones of kids who'd had cancer, or who'd been physically hurt by another person—the students held hands. *You and me. We share a thing the others don't. There may be only two of us, but I'm glad we aren't alone.*

I spent every summer of my early twenties leading activities like this at a small hippie camp in Massachusetts.

The image of walking across a room to join others like me never left my mind. Events would happen—wrecking my motorcycle, getting my heart broken, stealing groceries when I was too broke to pay for them—and I would see myself crossing the floor of the old camp rec hall toward a group of people to whom these same things had happened, and it gave me comfort. It was like emotional Red Rover.

Later, when I told my parents I was sober when I wasn't, in my mind I'd hear a young counselor blowing on a lifeguard whistle and saying, "Cross the room if you've ever lied about your drinking." In my mind I'd shuffle over to my people. Walking back to my studio apartment off Colfax after the last day of a job I needed but didn't like and never wanted, I'd hear the counselor again: "Cross the room if you've ever been fired." And then there was the day I missed my period. I heard the counselor say, "Cross the room if you ever had to borrow $300 to do the thing you never thought you would do, the thing that would destroy you and save you at the same time."

As I crossed that summer camp rec hall in my mind, I pictured myself walking past the rich women and the lucky women and the good women, and finally ending up at the latest group I belonged to: women who didn't have the $300. Your membership in this group is never revoked, even later in life, long after you get a real job and always have $300 for whatever you need. Just like you never get to not be the kid whose dad left when you were ten or the kid who skipped third grade, you never get to not be the girl who had to borrow the $300.

I had worked at the psychic call center for only two weeks when I realized that my period was late. I possessed no qualifications for the job—no special ability to see the future, no clairvoyance or second sight. What I did have one windy afternoon, when I bumped into an old friend on the street, was an empty bank account and an impatient landlord.

"Morgan!" I cheered, and hugged my former roommate and coworker. "It's been forever. Still waiting tables at the Pegasus?"

"Nope." She brushed her brown curls out of her face. "I'm working at a psychic phone line now."

"Shut up, Ms. Cleo," I said, assuming she was joking.

"No, for real," she said. "It's so easy. Hey, you could totally do it." Funny, I'd been told the same thing one week earlier by another friend who was stripping at PT's Topless.

Morgan cupped her hand around a Marlboro Light and lit it expertly, despite the wind.

We shared the cigarette and watched pedestrians jay-walk across Thirteenth Street as she told me about her job.

"They're basically always hiring, and the interview is just doing a 'reading' for the manager," Morgan said. "I can tell you exactly what to say. She had a terrible divorce two years ago and she keeps dating jerks, so just talk about that and she'll love you. Throw in something about archery and she'll hire you on the spot. She's obsessed with it." Morgan took the half-smoked cigarette back from me. "That's the job, when it comes down to it. Figuring out what people want to hear."

After a week of trying to learn tarot cards, I decided it was either that or stripping, and stripping called for tanning, shaving, and dieting. Both jobs required insight into desire, but I could read tarot cards in my pajamas, so the choice seemed obvious. I called Morgan's boss and set up a time for my test reading.

Nothing about the downtown Denver high-rise sig-naled that a psychic call center took up the ninth floor. No neon crystal ball, no "Call 1–800 . . ." sign. Even as you walked off the elevator and into the cubicle farm, the only hint of the supernatural was one heavily decorated work-space. Stacy, a woman my age who had been assigned to show me around, motioned toward the four-by-four cube that looked like the Grateful Dead had set up a booth at a Renaissance fair.

"That's Monique's cube," Stacy said. "She's been here *forever,* really believes in her 'powers,' and makes the company a lot of money. Anyway, you'll be assigned an empty desk and a phone each day when you start your shift."

But it turned out that I was no Monique. I didn't believe in my powers, and I'd overestimated my ability to stomach manipulating people for money. I assumed it would be the same as pretending to like guests I waited on at a restaurant, but smiling at a four-top of middle-aged women who had ordered just water and soup was one thing, and keeping a sad, recently divorced middle-aged man on the phone longer than he could probably afford was another. *Cross the room if you ever made money doing something dishonest.* That first check was small, but my rent was due. And two weeks later I realized my period was late.

I had a baby when I was thirteen. Not my own, but a stranger's.

Stephen became mine the first night my family brought him home. He was a foster baby, and I never wanted anyone else to hold him. Sometimes I'd unwrap him from the receiving blankets the adoption agency had given us, just to feel the warmth of his baby skin next to mine.

My mother, Peggy, warned me not to get too attached, since we couldn't keep him—but to absolutely no effect. I'd rush home after school hoping Stephen was awake from his nap.

"Don't wake him up just to hold him," Peggy would say. Then she'd find me in my room, a sleepy infant in my thin, young arms.

"He was already awake," I'd lie. He was my baby.

We fostered Stephen during a difficult time in my life. I felt alienated from basically everything except my cat and Stephen. Holding that perfect little infant in my arms, I felt deeply human and connected and entirely unjudged. To this day, whenever I hold a baby, I feel it is giving me once again a blessing of innocence, of what's possible, a slice of a moment when I am free of cynicism. Babies remind me that there is hope. They minister to me in a way nothing else can. They're preverbal love. Primordial priests wrapped in cotton.

I told my mom that I wanted to keep him because I loved him. But I also wanted to keep him so that he would love me back. Both things were true, but only one was said.

"Don't get too attached," she would repeat. But I volunteered to warm his bottles and mix the formula and feed him, just to feel his perfect weight in my arms, to hear the rhythmic sound of him sucking at the bottle. I knew my mother was watching me, concerned. She'd stand at a short distance and assess the sight of me, her sickly daughter, still sweaty from her run home from school, holding this perfect, healthy baby.

I, Peggy's own baby, had been born early and orange and in need of three immediate blood transfusions. I shouldn't have been conceived, much less born alive. Peggy had been on birth control, and she also had RH factor, a condition that causes a mother's body to react to the baby growing inside her. Nowadays there is a single shot that can be administered to women with her condition that makes it safe to carry and deliver a baby. But in the 1960s, women with RH factor could usually count on having only one healthy baby, because the condition grew worse with each subsequent birth. One baby was a blessing. Two was unlikely. Three was hardly possible.

Peggy had been sixteen when, at a church picnic on a cool summer afternoon, she spotted a tall, painfully thin man with black hair and light blue eyes. Peggy married Dick Bolz the week she turned eighteen. Within months they had moved to Germany for his first assignment in the U.S. Air Force. She was nineteen when my big sister, Barbara, was born, and they soon rolled the dice for a second baby—a boy, Gary, who arrived eighteen months later, after they'd moved to Texas. When she held her young, healthy, second-born child in her own young arms, the doctor in the San Antonio military hospital said, "Peggy, you must always be on birth control now. Forever."

Four years passed, and then she missed a period.

I love picturing her holding me in the military hospital in Pennsylvania, my color fresh for a few hours after a stranger's blood replaced all of my own. Peggy loves telling the story of how when I was one day old and the doctors still didn't know if I would live, a particularly bossy nurse had told her that she shouldn't put me to the breast. "You don't want your milk to come in when you probably won't have a baby to nurse," she'd said to Peggy.

Two days later, when I lived longer than expected and my mother was still breastfeeding me, the same nurse scolded her, "You're just going to make that baby sicker." To which Peggy, full of faith, prayer, and pure will, lifted up her head and said, "That just doesn't sound right to me," and switched me from one breast to the other.

On the drive home from the hospital, my mother asked my father if they could stop at an antique store she loved, the one in that old barn. A few weeks earlier, she'd seen a rocking chair hanging from the wall, the kind with runners that extend far behind it.

Her arms rested perfectly on the chair, and since I was already hungry again, she sat down, rocking farther back than any rocking chair ever should, and nursed me in that antique store under the hospital receiving blanket. My parents bought the chair and took it home with me.

Growing up, we three kids loved telling our guests to try out that rocking chair, knowing they would panic thinking they were going to tip all the way back. But they never did. It just felt like that.

One day, after mixing and warming Stephen's formula and coaxing a few droplets onto my forearm to check the temperature, I sat my bony butt down in that creaky rocking chair. Peggy sat across from me on the gold velvet sofa and watched as I fed Stephen. My twelve-year-old arms fell between the armrests of the chair, too short to rest on them directly, and I kissed the baby's small feet as he sucked contentedly on his bottle.

Peggy smiled at us. "She was so selfless," she said, clearly hoping that I'd ask her what she meant.

"Who?" I said, relenting.

"Stephen's birth mother. Don't ever judge her for giving him up, Nadia. That was a godly decision."

She'd told me this more than once, how noble Stephen's birth mom's decision had been, how selfless. His biological mother had thought of her baby and whoever his adoptive parents would be before thinking of herself.

Several weeks later, the afternoon finally arrived when I came home to find my mother holding Stephen and a small diaper bag in her arms. A suitcase sat by her side like a betrayal.

"He's been adopted!" she said, as if that were something to celebrate.

I begged her to keep him. Begged. "I'll do all the work, I promise." Who even were these people who presumed to be his parents? They didn't love him like I did. No one did. He was my baby.

I lacked the selflessness Peggy had praised in Stephen's birth mother then, and I lacked it eleven years later, when I was pregnant without wanting to be. *If you were selfless enough to give up a child for adoption, cross the room.* Stephen's mom could move forward, but I knew I could not.

If I couldn't give up someone else's baby, I never could have given up my own. And if I couldn't give up a baby and I couldn't keep a baby, then I just couldn't *have* a baby. I was the same age as my mom had been when she missed her period when she wasn't supposed to. But at 24, *I* wasn't married with two children. I was single, just two years clean and sober, and making $800 a month as a "psychic." I hadn't even seen a dentist for six years. I would have made a horrible single mother. I loved my boyfriend too much, but he loved me not enough—and although for a minute I thought maybe we would marry and start a real life, that's not what happened.

Stacy at the call center had given me the name and number of a doctor she herself had used the year before after a drunken one-night stand took a turn for the permanent. "The doctor's good," she said. "But not exactly warm."

Which is when I became the girl who had to borrow $300 to do the thing she had never thought she would do.

The morning after the abortion, I was lying on the thin mattress in the corner of my studio apartment. The mattress came from inside the only other piece of furniture I owned, a small and stained sleeper sofa, which now sank to the ground whenever you sat on it. The couch looked solid, but its insides had been pulled out of it. It was a body made of only skin and air.

My boyfriend, Eric, who'd been caring and affectionate and supportive through all of this, had left moments earlier for his job delivering pizzas. Suddenly, though, there was a knock on my door. I pulled myself up from the mattress. It was my friend Claire, a New Zealander who had overstayed her visa and survived on whatever cash she could make—cooking and sewing and creating all kinds of beauty out of scraps.

"I thought you might need a few things," she said when I opened the door. She handed me a basket lined with a vintage ladies' handkerchief and filled with fresh bread, homemade soup, a bar of dark chocolate, and two perfect tangerines.

Claire had visited several times before, so I hadn't thought to warn her again about the likelihood of being swallowed by my sofa. And so this sweet, nurturing moment of deep friendship was punctuated by Claire's skinny bum hitting the ground, her knees and torso meeting like two covers of a hardback book.

We broke into the kind of laugh that only people who are sad can manage.

Four years later, when I was in labor with Harper and scared out of my mind with pain and powerlessness, I calmed myself by repeating the words "Every human. Every human." It was something I'd thought a lot about during my pregnancy. Every human represents a pregnancy and a birth. What was happening to me and to my body seemed to me alien, violent. But women have been laboring and delivering their babies since the dawn of time, and on that night I joined them. They were waiting for me on the other side of this emotional Red Rover.

My baby had been waiting, too. The one I could keep. The one I would nurse in Peggy's antique rocking chair even though I would sometimes panic, thinking I might tip all the way back.

. . .

Sometimes I do the math. How old would the child be if I'd chosen differently? It's simple: add four years to Harper's age or six to Judah's.

My choice destroyed me for a time, though not because I thought I'd committed a horrible sin or because I felt ashamed. It was because I knew I would have loved that baby. That is true. But more than one thing can be true at a time, and what is also true, deeply true, is that even after I had children, even after I became a pastor, never once for a single minute did I regret my choice. It was the right one.

When Harper was born and I held her, and heard her small breath, it made me think of God. When babies emerge from the blood and oil of their mother's womb, when their skin touches air for the first time, the chilly shock of it opens their new mouth. And if they are to live, they must pull breath into their tiny lungs, those sacks of delicate wings feathered with blood vessels.

In some Muslim traditions, the very first thing a newborn baby hears is the name of God, whispered into the child's right ear by their father. I like to think of this as a way of reinforcing whose they are and from whom they came. Perhaps to whisper the name of God to a baby who just emerged from the womb is a way to say that the breath the baby just took is the breath of God, that it is from that very same divine source that the baby has come to us and it is to that divine source the baby will return after the last breath.

Rabbis have long written that the soul enters the body

at birth, with the first breath. For breath is the gift of life from the one who created us. From the God who is both our origin and our destination. And in the Hebrew Bible, YHWH (or Yahweh) is the four-letter name of God, too holy to be spoken, which is why instead in our Bibles it simply is replaced with "Lord."

But some rabbis teach that Yahweh is not even really a word at all. They say it is literally the sound of breath itself, which makes sense, since the closest translation of its meaning is "the One Who Causes to Become." "Then the Lord God formed the earthling from the dust of the ground, and breathed into their nostrils the breath of life; and the earthling became a living being" (Genesis 2:7).*

Inhale, *yah*. Exhale, *weh*. Inhale, *yah*. Exhale, *weh*.

I finished writing a draft of this story about pregnancy and babies and my mother's rocking chair while I was working on the teaching staff at a remote Lutheran retreat center in Washington State. It was summer. Harper would go off to college in the fall, and Judah was about to start a three-year apprenticeship, so we'd taken the opportunity to spend a week together in a place we loved.

When Harper finished reading the draft, she hugged me and nodded knowingly. Then we made our way down the hill from our cabin to the fireside room, where I was about to participate in a weekly faculty forum, a time in which the retreat center's teaching staff gathered to dis-

---

* Richard Rohr, *The Naked Now: Learning to See as the Mystics See* (Chicago: Crossroad, 2009), ch. 2.

cuss the wide range of topics we'd talked about in the days prior. About thirty-five folks sat before us to listen and ask questions.

For the next hour, we talked about ecology, liturgy, theology, and the conflict in Northern Ireland. Then, late in the faculty forum, a man in his early seventies spoke up. "There's only one thing no one mentioned this week, something I feel very strongly about."

I thought snarkily, *You understand that there are a lot of topics in the world, right? Like, we also never mentioned space travel or sea turtles or chicken gizzards.*

He continued regardless. "About a million Americans have died in combat since this country was founded. And we have days where we remember them and we honor them." His wife, who was seated next to him, elbowed him gently in the side, like a warning he chose not to heed.

"But hundreds of thousands of Americans die *every year* and no one even notices," he continued. "They are murdered. Murdered in the womb. Why didn't we talk about *that*?"

It was fight or flight for me at that point. I located the nearest exit. Had I not taken a moment to pray for help, I would have either walked out of the room or committed aggravated assault on a seventy-year-old man.

Instead, in my most measured voice, I spoke up. "Sir, the fact is, many of us hold a view that Christians and Jews have held for a very, very long time—that based on the creation story in Genesis, life begins with breath. So do not lob your accusations of murder at those whose premise is very different from yours."

I inhaled as deeply as I could, which wasn't that deep

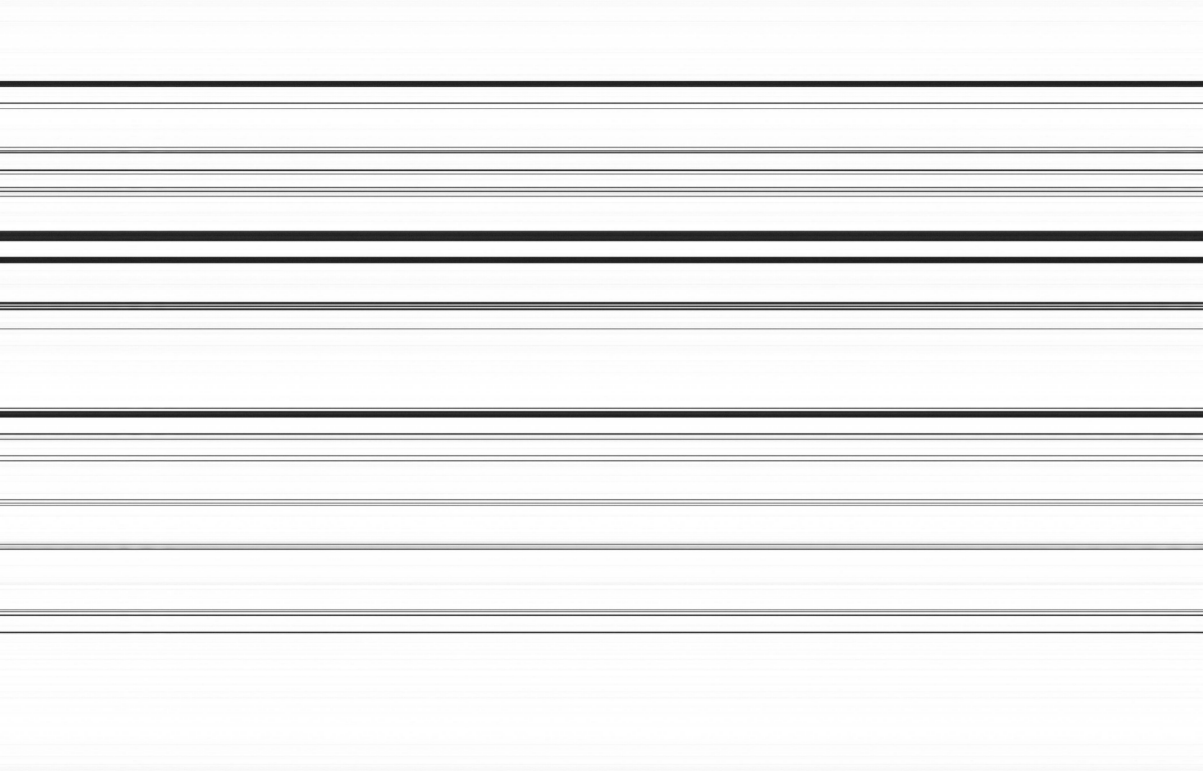

ad never said
tion when I

at day, about
one had de-
it, because I

he body lan-
ngry many of
se of what I'd
g said here in
have also had
would love to

ll to the din-
erbal tea, and
For hours we
about sex and
rt of the week

her woman ap-
was free.

lling me."
—two years ago,
my husband or

"I guess I never

I thanked her again
to maybe think about
Then I made my
boyfriend back home,
We'd been together fo
together once before, t
name is Eric. He used t

because I was angry. Then I said something I had never said in public. "And you know what? I had an abortion when I was twenty-four."

Then I told the story I had written just that day, about how I love babies and that choosing to not have one had destroyed me for a while and yet I never regretted it, because I knew it was the right decision for me.

I looked around the room and noticed the body language of the women, how tense and sad and angry many of them appeared. But I suspected it wasn't because of what I'd said. I added, "If you were hurt by something said here in this room today, then I am so sorry. And if you have also had an abortion and would like to talk about it, I would love to hear your story."

I was up until midnight.

A group of women made our way uphill to the dining hall, fixed ourselves toast and cups of herbal tea, and described our anger over the man's comment. For hours we laughed and drank tea and told our stories about sex and our bodies and pregnancy. It was the best part of the week for me.

As I walked back up to my cabin, another woman approached me, like she'd been waiting until I was free.

"I was twenty" was all she said.

I gave her a hug and said, "Thanks for telling me."

She cried, and I waited. "It was twenty-two years ago, and I have never told another person. Not my husband or mom or friends. No one."

When I asked her why, she simply said, "I guess I never felt invited to."

I thanked her again, hugged her again, and invited her to maybe think about telling a few more people.

Then I made my way back up the hill and texted my boyfriend back home, told him what had just happened. We'd been together for almost a year by then. We'd been together once before, too, back when I was twenty-four. His name is Eric. He used to deliver pizzas.

HOW ABORTION GOT ON THE EVANGELICAL POLITICAL AGENDA: A HISTORY

In 1968, *Christianity Today,* the flagship magazine for conservative Evangelicals, published a special feature on birth control. The article quoted Bruce Waltke, a professor from the famously conservative Dallas Theological Seminary, who said that the Bible plainly teaches that life begins at birth, not conception.

"God does not regard the fetus as a soul, no matter how far gestation has progressed," Waltke claimed. "The Law plainly exacts: 'if a man kills any human life he will be put to death (Leviticus 24:17). But according to Exodus 21:22–24, the destruction of the fetus is not a capital offense....Clearly then in contrast to the mother, the fetus is not reckoned as a soul.'"*

Physician Jonathan Dudley later wrote an opinion piece for CNN's Belief blog in which he noted that viewpoint was the "consensus among evangelical thinkers at the time."†

What changed? you might ask. Well, not the Bible, that's for sure. In 1969, several black families in Mississippi filed suit against private Christian schools that had excluded black students from enrolling. That's what changed.

---

* And in 1973, Robert L. Pettus Jr., a medical doctor, wrote a book titled *As I See Sex Through the Bible,* based on a series of classes he taught for his Church of Christ congregation in Madison, Tennessee. He painstakingly used scripture to determine the answer to questions about sexuality and gender roles, most conclusions adhering to the conservative Christian thinking of the day. But when discussing what the Bible said about abortion, he concluded that a fetus does not have a soul because it was with breath that God gave Adam life.

† Jonathan Dudley, "My Take: When Evangelicals Were Pro-Choice," Belief blog, CNN, October 20, 2012.

How is that lawsuit connected to views on abortion? When it comes to the Religious Right, the commonly held origin story is that in 1973 American Evangelicals woke from their political malaise as a response to *Roe v. Wade*. It's a compelling story, but it's not entirely true.[*] The issue that originally galvanized Evangelical Christian voters was one of "religious freedom"—namely, the freedom for Christian institutions to remain deeply racist.

Nine years before the suit against racist admission policies of Christian schools in Mississippi, Bob Jones Sr., an evangelist and the founder of the university that bears his name, claimed in a radio address that racial segregation was ordained by God, and that to oppose segregation was to oppose God and "God's plan" for humanity.[†] It would not be until 1971, forty-four years after its founding, that Bob Jones University would admit its first African American student, and even then only because the federal government forced its hand.[‡] That year, the U.S. Supreme Court ruled in *Coit v. Green* that private schools would be denied tax-exempt status if they maintained racially discriminatory policies.

Paul Weyrich, founder of the conservative think tank The Heritage Foundation and one of the architects of the Religious Right, wanted to further rally American Christians as a moral force on the stage of 1970s American politics. So after mobilizing to defend Bob Jones University and its racially discriminatory policies, he and several other Evangelical leaders held a conference call to discuss their strategy going forward.

---

[*] Randall Balmer, *Thy Kingdom Come: How the Religious Right Distorts Faith and Threatens America* (New York: Basic Books, 2006), Kindle ed., loc. 463–70.

[†] Daniel L. Turner, *Standing Without Apology: The History of Bob Jones University* (Greenville, SC: BJU Press, 2001), 225, 369.

[‡] It was not until 2000 that interracial dating was no longer banned on the campus of Bob Jones University.

The conversation is detailed by Dartmouth historian Randall Balmer in his book *Thy Kingdom Come*:

> Someone suggested...that they had the makings of a broader political movement—something that Weyrich had been pushing for all along—and asked what other issues they might address. Several callers made suggestions, and then, according to Weyrich, a voice on the end of one of the lines said, "How about abortion?" And that is how abortion was cobbled into the political agenda of the Religious Right.*

After rallying to defend the religious freedom for conservative Christian institutions to remain racist and still retain tax-exempt status, a small coalition of Evangelical leaders wanted to keep the momentum going, and decided the issue that could build their movement was abortion. That was the day Evangelicals started changing their minds around what the Bible says about when life begins.

There are so many varied experiences of conception and pregnancy. Some of us long to conceive and never do; some of us had babies we did not want; some of us miscarried babies we desperately wanted. How each person experiences conception and pregnancy differs according to their circumstances, beliefs, and desires.

By reminding you of this history—that Christians originally believed life began at birth and that the pro-life movement was contrived by political motivations—I do not wish to diminish or deny anyone's experience or perspective. I only wish to say that if the prevailing

---

* Balmer, *Thy Kingdom Come*, Kindle loc. 481–532.

Evangelical argument about abortion—that the Bible is "clear" that life starts at conception or in the womb, so anyone who is truly Christian must therefore believe what good Christians have "always" believed, that abortion is murder—has created shame within you, or if it kept you from terminating a pregnancy you wish you could have ended, or if it has caused you to harm yourself or others, or if it has kept you from voting your conscience, I want you to know the history of this position. And I want you to be free, because there are many ways to view the issue and remain faithful. There are many ways to read scripture and remain faithful. There are many ways to remain faithful.

THE FIREPLACE

"I remember in youth group, they had this metaphor about fire which they used all the time," he said, squinting in the sunlight after we'd walked out of Hooked on Colfax.

"The fireplace?" I asked, rolling my eyes.

He just laughed, pulling out his car keys. "Exactly."

Trent had just spent an hour describing what he learned as a kid from his church: how the only way to please God, the same being who created him with a sexuality to begin with, was to not engage with his erotic nature whatsoever. As if the God of the Universe had programmed into creation a passive-aggressive test of our willpower.

He is just one of many people who've told me tales of manipulative youth group teachings about the danger of sex, teachings they received in lieu of comprehensive sex education.

There's the rose that's passed around a circle, representing a girl's sexual virtue. Each boy in the group pulls a petal off so that by the end, her husband only has a dried-up stem.

Then there's the glass of water each person spits in, and the last person in line is asked if they want to drink it now that everyone else's body fluids are mixed with the water. And then there's the fire metaphor.

Fire, abstinence proponents tell kids, can be safe and warm and comforting—but only when you contain it. Take fire outside of the fireplace, and it will consume everything around it. Sex works in the same way. If you don't confine it to the "fireplace" of a lifelong, monogamous, heterosexual, Christian marriage, it will burn you and destroy everything in your life.

Here's the thing. I can't say that sex is unlike fire. It is an apt metaphor. However, fire is an essential part of human existence. It's dangerous, yes, but it is not unmanageable. There are fireplaces, fine. But fire also shows up in Bic lighters. And gas stoves, and hot water heaters, and in rings at campsites, and on a billion birthday cake candles. Not to mention the sun.

Driving is dangerous, so we teach our kids as much as we can about it, and then we hand them the keys. Chopping vegetables is dangerous, so we teach our children how to properly hold a knife and bend their knuckles just so. Friendships are dangerous, so we teach our children about generosity, boundaries, and self-esteem.

And fire is dangerous, so we teach them to respect it. Yet I don't know anyone who has not been burned in some way, whether by a hot frying pan, a Fourth of July sparkler, or a curling iron. It hurts, and we heal. Of course, there are those who have been burned so badly, the scars never actually disappear. All of these things are true about fire. And so many things are also true about sex.

Sex can bring warmth, but it can also be chilling. Sex can bring connection and also alienation. Sex can provide insight but sometimes confusion. Sex can empower but sometimes humiliate. And we can teach our kids that every single one of these things is possible in and out of marriage. In straight and in queer relationships. In the young and in the old. Sex shines and flickers, and it rages, lights, warms, and burns.

Eventually Trent no longer accepted that sex was a sin, and he wanted to take a crack at it for himself. But as he started going on dates, he found it difficult to access his sensual nature—he didn't know how to be sexually forward with a woman, to be sexually expressive with her. Long after he'd rejected the teachings of his youth, Trent felt as if the erotic and sexual response systems that we all naturally have, and which his church had encouraged him to ignore, had atrophied in him. He worried the damage that had been done would be permanent.

In 1986, I was seventeen years old, and despite my church's best efforts, I had sex. Outside the fireplace.

My boyfriend, Jeff, was twenty, and shockingly experienced for someone his age. He loved women. He loved female bodies and loved giving and receiving pleasure. He was a gentle, considerate, and very generous lover. I'm one of the lucky few who gets to say that my introduction to sex was amazing, and with someone I loved. Jeff wasn't a

Christian, but he did not settle for just consent and mutuality. He showed concern. A few weeks after we started dating, and before we ever had sex, he took me to Planned Parenthood so we could have reliable birth control.

Sex was *good*.

Yet I had to keep it a secret. I couldn't tell anyone; not my parents or other kids at church, and I sure as hell couldn't confide in my pastor. So, like most Christian kids who become sexually active, I navigated my sexuality without any wisdom from my elders, because everyone who was older in my life adhered to the idea that "all sex outside of marriage is a sin." The last thing I wanted was for someone to "speak truth in love" by telling me to stop having sex. I didn't need a well-intentioned rebuke. What I needed, like my parishioner Cecilia, was wisdom about sexual relationships.

Sex wasn't ruining my whole life like the church had said it would. I wasn't hurting anyone. I wasn't hurting myself or Jeff. But the message was clear: my sexuality and my spirituality could not inhabit the same space. So I started lying about where I was and what I was doing, and I spent less time at church.

It was 2012, and I was on the phone with the organizers of my denomination's National Youth Gathering, which would be held later that summer at the Superdome and at which I would be speaking on the main stage. I mused, "I wish I had a Magic 8 Ball that could offer me the answer to one question: 'How many STDs and unplanned pregnancies have occurred in the last twenty-five years as a result of sexual contact between teenagers at the ELCA's National Youth Gatherings?'"

Now, the ELCA is one of the most progressive-minded denominations in the country. We ordain gay folks and have teaching statements on the sins of mass incarceration and global warming. I think of us as being a church that embraces reality. "So how great would it be," I said, "if our denomination's national Youth Gathering had a place in the resource area where adults stood by, ready to provide sound information about sexual health?" So many of these kids come from areas of the country where the only information available to them is about abstinence.* This could be their only chance to get the guidance they need. I added, "If you guys can't provide these resources to the youth of our church, my own congregation would be willing to . . . you know, at our expense." I paused, but they were pretty quiet on the other line.

A no-brainer, right? The reply came weeks later.

"We talked about it. It's a great idea, but the parents wouldn't stand for it."

I couldn't stop thinking about that. What, exactly, would the parents not stand for? Was it the fact that some of their teenagers were sexually active, something the ELCA had nothing to do with? Or the fact that the church would dare

---

* Abstinence education does not prevent teen pregnancy; education on contraception use prevents teen pregnancy. A study showed that improved contraceptive use is responsible for 86 percent of the decline in the U.S. adolescent pregnancy rate between 1995 and 2002. J. Santelli et al., "Explaining Recent Declines in Adolescent Pregnancy in the United States: The Contribution of Abstinence and Improved Contraceptive Use," *American Journal of Public Health* 97 (2007): 3.

to acknowledge it, and help to ensure the health and safety of their kids? Statistically, it's unlikely that rules against providing guidance on sexual health do anything to keep teenagers from having sex. In a study published in the June 2017 *Journal of Pediatrics*, researchers found that teen pregnancy rates are 40–50 percent higher than the national average in areas of Texas where abstinence-only education is the law.

So I started wondering: what is it within parents that gets in the way of us embracing reality? Do we honestly believe that Jesus was as shocked and dismayed about sex as the church seems to be? Really?

If we're honest with ourselves, we could very quickly answer why parents and the church have so often obsessed over teenagers and sex: fear.

Yes, sex has its dangers.* It would be foolish to suggest otherwise. Obviously, as parents, we are afraid of our children making a temporary choice with a permanent consequence, a moment of pleasure followed by a lifetime of sickness or premature parenthood. And more simply, we don't want our children to experience heartbreak or use sex the way I have used sex at different points in my own life— namely, as a way to medicate loneliness, or to feel worthy. These are all reasonable fears.

---

* Respected sex therapist Esther Perel said in an interview with Patty Olwell, "In the U.S., sex is the risk factor. In Europe, being irresponsible is the risk factor. Sex is natural and part of human development. That's the fundamental difference of the kind of education we get. And I think the U.S. can do better." (*Therapist Uncensored* podcast, episode 46, "Redefining Infidelity," 38:30). American adults who support abstinence-only education for children and teens are being irresponsible.

But maybe I as a parent also fear the *mystery* of sex, because I know how I myself have been swallowed whole by desire, how I have lost myself in a connection with my lover in a way that is terrifying, a way that I cannot control or even define. I know that when I see my lover, something within me uncoils. That which has been contained—by social convention and protective psychology and basic clothing for most of my adult life and most of my waking hours—quickens from within. It is a wildness, part velvet, part forest fire. A wildness that desires in equal parts to consume and caress. Desire is tricky. It is destruction and insistence and risk and the goddamn Easter bunny, all at once. It makes every edge blur like a thumb run over a charcoal line.

Sex can be procreative, a way of creating new life. It can be intimate, a way for love to be expressed between partners. It can be revelatory, a way in which we discover ourselves and another. It can be boring, mind-blowing, or regrettable. It can be a beautiful aspect of human flourishing, and it can be a humiliating aspect of human degradation. It can be the safest place we can go or the most dangerous thing we can do. It can be obligation or joy. It can be deadly. It can be life.

Given all of this, maybe it makes sense that we reach for some rules. Rules can be helpful, of course. Society has to function, and humans can be pretty horrible to each other. We steal each other's shit and try to hide money from the government so that we don't have to pay our share. We simply cannot rely on everyone being good. This is why we have laws—whether passed by government or intuited through social norms.

But religious law can never keep us as safe as we think it will. For instance, telling teenagers—those wild, beautiful, insane beings filled with hormones—that they must abstain from sex and never think about sex is seldom effective. And even when it does work, there can be harsh consequences. When our teenagers do manage to shut down their own sexual responses and desires, they can be left later in their lives, like Trent was, trying to connect frayed wires, strangers to themselves as sexual beings.

The main thing accomplished through these efforts is that adults feel like we are *doing* something. We think we are protecting them. We think we are keeping them safe from harm. We think we are keeping them pure. And these are noble instincts. But what we're more likely doing is projecting our own bullshit onto our kids—the fear of our own desires, the peer pressure and cultural norms of our religious community. We are stunting our children by withholding the tools and the wisdom they need for a healthy sexual future, or we are sending them straight to their peers or the internet for guidance.

In 1979, my mother handed me a mint-green book, *Wonderfully Made*, the cover of which bore the cartoonish image of four brunette males on the top and four blond females on the bottom, shown from the youngest to the oldest, from the smallest to the biggest. At every age and size, the white boy holds a football in his arm, but only the youngest girl on the cover is jumping rope; the older females walk empty-handed. A parade of gender norms, marching into my life with a one-size-fits-all message of "God's plan" for sex and marriage. She told me to let her know if I had any questions. This was the extent of the "sex talk" I received from my parents.

I wanted to do better when I had kids. And yet, when it was my turn to have the "sex talk" with my own, I had no idea how to do it, either. Here, have a look:

2006: I mean to have "the talk" with Harper.

2007: I mean to have "the talk" with Harper.

2008: I mean to have "the talk" with Harper *and* Judah.

2009: The kids' dad and I buy them each a book, hand it to them, and tell them to come to us if they have questions.

For all my big talk now about the things we can teach our children about sex, *this* was the extent of the "sex talk" I gave my kids when they were young.

Maybe you, too, defaulted to this with your own kids, even though you wanted to do better. If so, you are not alone. Maybe you felt like I did: afraid. I was afraid of being uncomfortable and of making my kids uncomfortable. Afraid of telling them too much too soon. It's hard to embrace the sexuality of our kids.

But by the time my kids were teenagers, I was determined to do better. And I did, somewhat. It wasn't easy. But it also wasn't impossible.

The year Harper was a high school senior, she and I were

driving to the grocery store when she looked up at me and said, "Justin has condoms, Mom. I just thought you should know." This was the matter-of-fact way that my daughter informed me she was having sex with her boyfriend.

I tried to not freak out. After all, she was older than I'd been with Jeff.

"Can I stay the night at his house Friday?" she asked. "His mom is fine with it, and she'll be home and everything."* Harper had been hanging out at their house a lot already, and I trusted her. But suddenly I couldn't access the forward-thinking, sex-positive woman who wanted teenagers to be given sex ed at a youth event.

It took a while to answer. I had so many thoughts to sort through. I thought about how I loved Justin. He was sweet and quirky, with his red hair and canvas sneakers covered in images of dinosaurs and his backpack that looked like Captain America's shield. He was a-dork-able, and a really good kid.

And yet my first thought about her staying the night was . . . no.

But if I said no, I thought, Harper might just defy me and do it anyway. Maybe she would do as I'd done, and follow her heart and not her mother. All because I couldn't accept the reality of her developing life. If I said yes, then at

---

* For a fascinating book on how most Americans oppose the idea of their teens sleeping over at their boyfriend's/girlfriend's house, while Dutch parents with the same educational background and socioeconomic status do not, and why, see Amy T. Schalet's book *Not Under My Roof: Parents, Teens, and the Culture of Sex* (Chicago: University of Chicago Press, 2011).

least we were communicating, and I would know where she really was that night.

Still, I thought, *What if people find out that I am letting my eighteen-year-old daughter sleep over at her boyfriend's house? That's just trashy. I might as well buy her a carton of Camels and half a dozen scratch tickets.*

But I didn't say that. Instead, I looked at Harper and said, "Go ahead. And thanks for asking me."

"We need milk" was all she said as we walked into the store. She was fine.

I was a mess.

We pulled up to our house after loading the car with groceries for the week, and I turned off the ignition and looked at her. I wanted more for her than just a green light from her mom, more than consent. She deserved *concern*.

"I want you to love sex, sweetie," I said to her as earnestly as I could manage while still sounding matter-of-fact about it. "I want you to be comfortable in your body and learn what it desires and how to communicate that to your lovers. So start that process now. Know your body. Speak up for what you want or don't want. That will serve you your whole life." When I said this, I almost choked up, thinking about the teddy bear in our kitchen with the balled up Post-its for breasts. I wanted for Harper now what I wanted for her then, to be safe and free and unselfconscious in her body.

I took a breath, holding back tears. She looked me straight in the eye. No shame, not even embarrassment. It gave me the strength to continue. "I want you to choose well, and to treat your lovers with respect and concern. And

I hope for your faith to be a part of your sexuality and vice versa. Also, you know that high you feel with Justin? It's the most amazing feeling in the world. But I want you to understand that if it goes badly or if and when you break up, there may be a commensurate low. And it will feel awful. But that doesn't mean something is wrong. It's just inescapable, and it will teach you important things about yourself." I thought for a second. "And one more thing," I finally said. "Pee afterward. I don't want you to get a UTI."

She laughed and did the typical teenager eye roll. "I knooooow!" she joked.

"I love you, baby. And I trust you."

Eighteen months later, in the summer of 2018, my son, Judah, spent a week away from home with thirty thousand other teenagers at the ELCA's Youth Gathering in Houston. There in the brightly lit, high-ceilinged exhibition hall, amid the World Hunger Appeal display, the acoustic music stage, the adult-size Big Wheel track, and the pizza vendors, was a small table from a little church in Denver staffed by professional sex educators.

They said yes this time.

WHO TOLD YOU YOU WERE NAKED?

WE DON'T REALLY know if all the animals could talk back then, or if for some reason it was just the snake. But the snake was a crafty motherfucker. He wanted to stir up some shit, so in an epic display of triangulation, he decided to gossip with Eve about God.

Like an episode of *Real Serpents of Eden County*, he slithered up to her and was like, "Honey, you know I totally love you, right? I mean that's like, the *only* reason I'm saying this, but did God really say you weren't allowed to eat from one of these here trees? I mean, did God really say that to you?"

Eve replied, "Well, kind of, I guess. I mean, we can eat of any tree; God just said there was that one in the middle that we can't eat from, and—this is weird—we can't even touch it. Or else we'll die."

The serpent saw his opening. "Shut up! God said that? I mean, I know you guys are friends, but girl, you totally won't die. God only said that because God knows that if you eat from that tree you would be like God, knowing good from evil. It actually makes me feel sorry for God, you know?"

Eve saw that the tree of knowledge of good and evil was beautiful and the fruit tasty and the wisdom it promised desirable. She ate the fruit—and, just to be clear, her unbelievably passive husband, who doesn't do or say shit, ate it, too. Rather than living in the freedom God gave them to just be who they were, they listened to a voice other than God's, and they believed the serpent and traded life for knowledge of good and evil.

The moment they ate of the fruit of the tree of knowledge of good and evil, their eyes were opened and the freedom of life—the freedom of just being with God as God's created beings, allowing God to be God and we to be they who are in need of God—vanished.

Which is the exact moment the idea of "nakedness" was introduced. Before then it didn't exist. But now the humans covered their bodies out of shame. Which is exactly how shame operates: it makes us hate our bodies, it obscures the image of God within us, it makes us hide, it makes us afraid of God, it makes us blame others.

The next day, God was just kind of strolling around the garden and realized the earthlings were nowhere to be found.

So God called out, "Hey, where are you guys?"

But they were hiding.

Before the weight of good and evil and the legalistic bullshit that has forever plagued religion entered into the minds and hearts of human beings, there was no shame—no shame about our bodies, or what those bodies desired, or how those bodies looked. There was absolutely no reason to hide from God.

But rather than just be with God as we were created, the humans chose to try to be *like* God, and that shit has not stopped to this day. We love taking our so-called knowledge of what is good and what is evil, of who is good and who is evil, and applying that to ourselves and to others like we are God.

The very first expression of shame was over our naked, sexual bodies. And since then, we earthlings have tried to define and control and condemn human sexuality.

Shame has an origin, and it is not God. When Adam and Eve tried to avoid God, God said, "Where are you?" And they said, "We were naked and tried to hide from you because we were afraid." God then said to them: "Wait. Who told you you were naked?"

Who told them they were naked? My money is on the snake. For some reason God allows us to live in a world where alternatives to God's voice exist, and those alternatives are where shame originates.

Maybe you, too, are hiding, having listened to a voice other than God's. But can you hear God saying, "Wait. Who told you you were naked? Who told you that you have to lie to be accepted? Who told you your body is not beautiful and worthy to be loved? Who told you that your sexual expression is something to be ashamed of? Who told you that?"

My money is on the snake. And he's a damned liar.

I SMELL SEX AND CANDY

[God is] a hedonist at heart. All those fasts and vig-
ils and stakes and crosses are only a façade. Or only
like foam on the seashore. Out at sea, out in His
sea, there is pleasure, and more pleasure. He makes
no secret of it; at His right hand are "pleasures for
evermore." Ugh! . . . He's vulgar, Wormwood. He
has a bourgeois mind. He has filled His world full
of pleasures. There are things for humans to do all
day long without His minding in the least—sleeping,
washing, eating, drinking, making love, playing,
praying, working. Everything has to be *twisted*
before it's any use to us. We fight under cruel disad-
vantages. Nothing is naturally on our side.

—One devil speaking to another in C. S. Lewis,
The Screwtape Letters

I was always a little afraid of my grandmother Helen. She
insisted on being called "Grandmother," never "Grandma"

or "Grannie." She was a good woman, but not terribly warm.

I recently asked my big sister if she thought Grandmother Helen ever experienced joy. "I think a clean kitchen gave her joy," she answered, and I tend to agree. She scrubbed the floors of her tiny kitchen every single day with her small arthritic hands.

As a girl, I would sometimes watch Grandmother scoot a stool up to the avocado-colored refrigerator and reach with her knobby hand for a white box on top. She would remove what looked like a caramel, unwrap it, and pop it in her mouth. I remember multiple times feeling a sting of betrayal that she wasn't sharing. But my mother explained that Grandmother's caramel-looking thing wasn't candy, it was a weight loss aid.

Ayds dietary candies were a popular appetite suppressant in the 1970s and early 1980s. They were taken off the market for obvious reasons. If you Google "Ayds dietary candies," you'll find old television ads that feature unfortunate lines like "Why take diet pills when you can enjoy Ayds?" and "Ayds helps you lose weight safely and effectively!"

The main ingredient in Ayds was benzocaine, a chemical that dulled the taste buds. (Looks like candy, tastes like Orajel.) For my grandmother and many women of her generation, the lure of sugar, the pleasure of actual candy, was so fraught with danger that they ate fake candy and then washed it down with a can of saccharin-laden Fresca.

Looking back, I want to simply dismiss as a neurotic eccentricity my grandmother's habit of avoiding the pleasure of actual food by eating a local anesthetic, but I suspect there is more to it than that. I learned early that our relationship to pleasure is *complicated.*

Theologically speaking, we were endowed by our creator with the capacity both to desire and to experience pleasure. It didn't have to be that way, and yet God gave us this gift. Consider, if you will, the humble clitoris, that magical bundle of nerve endings whose only biological function is to provide sexual pleasure for women. Unlike the penis, which is a multitasker, the clitoris literally has no other function but pleasure.

Our taste buds explode with pleasure at the first bite of chocolate cake, and this gift is from God. "He has filled his world with pleasures," as the demon from C. S. Lewis's *Screwtape Letters* insists. As with cake, so with sex.

As Sam and I drank coffee at Hooked on Colfax late one morning, he described the messages he had received throughout his teens. Every Wednesday night, Sam's youth group met in a darkened gymnasium dressed up as a rock concert: decorative fabrics, professional sound equipment, and a light show. A thin, attractive youth pastor with a soul patch and skinny jeans would deliver a message about the evils of sex, drugs, and alcohol.

In Matthew's Gospel, Jesus says, "You have heard that it was said, 'You shall not commit adultery.' But I say to you that everyone who looks at a woman with lust has already committed adultery with her in his heart." This was a favorite verse of Sam's youth pastors, who wielded it to warn kids against even *thinking* about sex. If lusting after a woman was just as bad as committing adultery, their logic held, then even thinking about sex is a sin.

"The weird thing," Sam told me, "was that it wasn't date rape or sexual harassment or even treating people disrespectfully that they were worried about. It was 'impure thoughts' and lust."

There are two problems that I see here: one, these were teenagers, whose bodies are designed to become sexual, and two, the Greek word for lust, *epithymia*, is about general desire, not thinking sexual thoughts. If *epithymia* was a term for sexual desire, it would make some other things Jesus said super weird. (For example, Luke 22:15: "And he said to them, I have had *sexual thoughts* about eating this Passover with you before I suffer.")

Like Sam, I was taught as a child that the Ten Commandments—and, really, all the rules in the Bible, plus several the church just kind of made up—were there because God loves us and wants us to be happy. But in Lutheran seminary I learned that the Ten Commandments are more about the fact that God loves our neighbors and wants to protect them from us. When Martin Luther took away the *Thou shall not murder* free space in the middle of our moral bingo card, he was taking his cue from Jesus. In this text from Matthew, Jesus is saying that *Thou shall not commit adultery* is not simply a matter of not screwing someone other than your spouse.* He's saying, once again, "Love

---

* For those who are interested in really learning about the causes of infidelity, I'd strongly suggest reading Esther Perel's *The State of Affairs: Rethinking Infidelity* (New York: HarperCollins, 2017).

your neighbor. People aren't objects. Let's not cause each other harm."

Nevertheless, Sam would sit in the gymnasium-turned-low-budget-pop-concert, listening to warnings against sexual thoughts and indulging in fantasy. Pornography, in particular, was condemned via a "God knows what websites you visit in the dark" type of admonishment.

"There was always a hint of 'If you continue a pattern of sin [in which you look at pornography], you're not a real Christian,'" he explained to me over the sounds of heavily caffeinated mothers trying to quiet their sugar-filled toddlers. "All of these messages worked together to convince me that my faith wasn't real because I 'struggled' with sexual desire."

But I'm here to tell you: unless your sexual desires are for minors or animals, or your sexual choices are hurting you or those you love, those desires are not something that you need to "struggle with." They are something to listen to, make decisions about, explore, perhaps have caution about. But struggle with? Fight against? Make enemies of? No.

Like Trent, Sam shut down a part of himself in order to please God. He disconnected from his body and his desires, and it backfired. Eventually Sam found it difficult to connect with even his own feelings, express them, and be heard by those closest to him. In the absence of these vital, intimate connections, he turned to porn to numb the pain.

Sam now considers himself a porn addict.

In my pastoral work I've started to suspect that the more someone was exposed to religious messages about control-ling their desires, avoiding sexual thoughts, and not lusting in their hearts, the less likely they are to be integrated physically, emotionally, sexually, and spiritually. I've also noticed that the less integrated physically, emotionally, sexually, and spiritually someone is, the more pornography they tend to consume. This is anecdotal evidence and not a scientific study.* Nonetheless, I'd like to congratulate conservative Christians on their success in bolstering an industry that they claim to despise.

Perhaps something similar would happen if we repeatedly told kids the same thing about chocolate: "Chocolate is very delicious, and God made chocolate to be enjoyed, but it is safe for us to eat only after we have found the one person God intended for us to enjoy chocolate with. Until then, God wants you to avoid temptation and control your desire for chocolate's deliciousness. The devil is going to do everything he can to convince you how delicious chocolate is, so make sure you don't watch movies where people are eating chocolate. And girls, boys want chocolate more than you

---

* However, there *are* scientific studies that show the importance developmentally of allowing adolescents to navigate their sexuality: "Beginning with puberty, the developmental transitions in brain networks involved in motivation, reward, and social-emotional processing likely create a unique inflection point for romantic love and sexual arousal to be experienced as positive rewards. A primary goal for adolescents is to learn how to engage in and navigate romantic and sexual relationships. In addition, these early romantic relationships have important implications for identity development, learning about sexual behavior, and future relationship trajectories. Parents, clinicians, and educators can provide relevant learning opportunities in this area, but at the same time, the majority of relevant learning comes from personal experience." A. B. Suleiman et al., "Becoming a Sexual Being: The 'Elephant in the Room' of Adolescent Brain Development," *Developmental Cognitive Neuroscience* 25 (2017): 209–20.

do, so don't wear shirts that might make boys think about chocolate. Chocolate is dangerous. Delicious, but dangerous. Don't even *think* about it."

I'd bet my life savings that if we did this, kids everywhere would be like "OMG, I gotta get some chocolate!" They'd make fake online profiles and order chocolate on the internet. They'd compulsively watch videos of people eating chocolate in increasingly disturbing ways. They'd grow numb to their hunger for real food. They'd binge on cheap chocolate—like, Palmer chocolate, you know? That, or they would sever themselves from their ability to know if they even want chocolate, or how to ask for it, or in what form chocolate suits them.

There is nothing wrong with the fact that our bodies are created to experience pleasure. There is nothing wrong with the fact that our bodies are stimulated by sexual stories and images. It's an empathic response. And just as humans have eaten sweets since the dawn of time, so, too, have human beings created erotic images as soon as we figured out how to scratch them on the insides of caves.

But what was different a generation ago was that we didn't have access to things like Slurpees and Porn Hub. Both the sweets and the sex available to us 24/7 today are exponentially more condensed in form and more convenient to access than anything our ancestors could have imagined. And I wonder if the cost of this, among other things, is a *loss* of pleasure, not an abundance of it. Can we enjoy the pleasure of our middle-aged spouse's body after consuming two straight hours of internet porn featuring impossibly perfect,

hairless, willing, youthful actors? How do we appreciate the
sweetness of an apple after consuming thirty-two ounces of
Mountain Dew?*

Alain de Botton, the atheist philosopher I referenced earlier, has written compellingly on the matter: "A brain originally designed to cope with nothing more tempting than an
occasional glimpse of a tribesperson across the savannah is
lost with what's now on offer on the net at the click of a but-
ton: when confronted with offers to participate continuously
in scenarios outstripping any that could be dreamt up by
the diseased mind of the Marquis de Sade. There is nothing
robust enough in our psychological make-up to compensate
for developments in our technological capacities."† In the
age of high-fructose corn syrup and internet porn, I wonder
sometimes if we've lost the capacity to understand pleasure
as we were created to experience it.

Here's what I know about the list that the great C. S.
Lewis put in the mouth of one of his characters ("sleeping,
washing, eating, drinking, making love, playing, praying,
working"): Every last one of these things is morally neutral.
Every last one of those activities can cause harm if overdone.
And every last one can also bring joy. Too much sleep and
your life falls apart; too little and you cannot function. Too
much washing and you end up with OCD and raw skin; too
little and you smell. Too much praying and you forget to

---

*   A topic worth exploring elsewhere is the financial aspect of both porn
and sugar. Who is making money on both of these things, and in what ways
are we as consumers being manipulated into compulsive consumption of
both?

†   Alain de Botton, "Why Most Men Aren't Man Enough to Handle Web
Porn," Speakeasy blog, *Wall Street Journal*, December 26, 2012.

actually take action; too little and you forget that there is a power greater than yourself. Too much making love and you could get sore (and also the dishes never get done, and there isn't time to long for sex again); too little and . . . what?*

So, how do human beings with our dual natures (being simultaneously sinner and saint) navigate a world full of pleasure when we so easily fall off either end of the abstinence-indulgence continuum? Well, perhaps we should consider what our theology of pleasure is. Because, friend, I do not believe God is monitoring your ability to steer clear of life's pleasures. Viewing sexually explicit images doesn't have to be harmful, just like eating cake doesn't have to be harmful.[†] But there *is* potential harm in both, and the harm varies according to who we are individually: our wiring, our histories, our relationships.

I do not know why some people can drink half a beer and call it a night. Twenty-six years of sobriety and I still find myself staring at the remaining booze in their glass wondering how they could possibly be so foolish. I would never have left a drop. There have been plenty of times I've contemplated grabbing the unfinished beer and doing it justice.

---

* Is there a cost to too little sex? For some, yes. But with caveats. Some people are truly asexual, in that they do not have a desire for genital contact, and yet they are still sexually embodied people who can and do experience pleasure and connection in other ways. Also, there are people who choose celibacy and indeed consider it a gift.

† I have parishioners who have told me that viewing pornography has actually helped them in their process of self-discovery. It allows them to have a curiosity about themselves. Why do some images stimulate them and some do not? And how might this information be useful in their sexual relationship with their partner?

But if I were to drink that remaining eight ounces of beer, a little switch would flip in me, and no matter the consequences, no matter how much I knew it would most certainly end badly, I would continue to drink, most likely until I passed out. I also don't know why I can eat four french fries and stop when my friend Sophie cannot. Same with video games. And exercise. And nail biting.

Some of us can eat a piece of chocolate cake once a month, enjoy the pleasure of it, and then immediately return to our balanced diet. But if you find that when you eat chocolate cake a switch gets flipped and suddenly you have no taste for anything else, to the extent that you desire only cake, cake might not be for you. Still, I will not sit here and say that no one should ever eat cake and that it destroys people's lives, just like I would never say that people should not drink because alcohol destroyed my life. Or that no one should ever view erotic imagery because Sam has developed destructive behaviors around it.

Problems can absolutely arise from the consumption of pornography, including sexual partners' feelings of betrayal and compulsive behaviors that inhibit healthy sexual activity.* (Not to mention that there are serious issues of consent, dignity, and justice in the porn industry.) Some people can watch porn and still have a very real and intimate connection with their partner; for them, watching it together doesn't diminish or disrespect their relationship. I have heard this story in my parish. Others have to steer clear

---

* To learn another perspective on the effects of pornography, see Pamela Paul, *Pornified: How Pornography Is Transforming Our Lives, Our Relationships, and Our Families* (New York: Times Books, 2005).

entirely. For them, just a few moments of porn and they cannot stop no matter all the reasons they can conjure to control themselves, and their compulsion causes insecurity in their partner and intimacy problems in their relationship. I have also heard *this* story in my parish.

I have no answers here. But what I will not do is pick the low-hanging fruit of moral outrage about porn that comes from both liberals and conservatives. Not while the consumption of pornography is so ubiquitous. I suspect a Venn diagram of those who express disgust about porn (either for reasons of justice or for reasons of sexual morality) and those who secretly watch porn would show a significant overlap. Expressing one thing and doing another is a fearful, lonely place to be, and as a pastor, I have no interest in adding to the shame so many people already have about porn, especially those who feel that they should "know better." I believe we can apply an ethic of concern here by acknowledging the potential harm without shaming the behavior entirely.

The point is, it all calls for *attention*. Does something enhance my life and relationships, or does it take it over? Is my behavior compulsive? When I or my partner experience this pleasure, is it bringing me or my partner more deeply into the moment, into the sacred, into our bodies, or is it separating one or both of us from these things?

I believe that our ability to experience pleasure in general, sexual and culinary specifically, is a gift from God, but I am also aware of how tricky these gifts are, and how easily twisted they can be, as Screwtape would say—twisted into dangerous things we avoid (thus eating benzocaine-laced "diet candy" and trying to not even *think* sexual thoughts) or into pain-numbing things we gratuitously gorge upon (thus shame-eating an entire cheesecake or streaming *Edward Penishands*).

As a pastor, I find myself concerned for the self-hatred Sam described, and I wonder how we could begin to honor sexual pleasure as something that can connect us more deeply to ourselves and others and God, yet still speak the truth about the ways in which our behaviors around sex can also do the opposite. Perhaps we could start by remembering what St. Paul wrote in 1 Corinthians: that all things are lawful but not all things are beneficial.

To begin with, I think the church could be a place that bravely encourages a healthy exploration into what the erotic actually is, at its best. The erotic can be that which opens us, peeling away our protective layer. Like citrus, there's a juicy, delicious part of us, which if always exposed may wither. That's what the erotic accesses in us. The peel is there for a reason. There's nothing wrong with it. I cannot move through the world without protecting the parts of me that are the sweetest and most vulnerable. But the erotic can be the way in which the smell of a lover's neck exposes something in us, like a thumbnail making the first opening into the skin of a tangerine. The vascular and the venial become one, and our breath itself changes. The erotic exposes complex layers of surface area: psyche, heart, body, desire, beauty.

Jesus, we know, was accused of being a drunkard and a glutton, a friend of prostitutes and tax collectors. His first miracle was to keep the wine flowing at a party he was attending. So the guy was not afraid of pleasure. But he also fasted for forty days in the desert and would often go to a mountain to pray alone. He seemed to live an integrated life of feasting *and* fasting.

As we look at pleasure, it may seem obvious at this point to suggest balance in all things. But I myself am lousy at moderation. I don't do anything a *little* bit. My friend Heather jokes that I have only two speeds: go and stop. So I do not propose another form of balance.

I once sat in my spiritual director Jane's office and lamented that I felt like the whole balance thing—where we are supposed to be able to do and have it all if we just maintain perfect equilibrium—is another form of bullshit pop spirituality that society made up to try to make me feel bad about myself.

"Maybe so," she said, patient as always. "Maybe 'rhythm' is a better word." With her palm, Jane patted her knee in a gentle cadence. "Can you find a maintainable rhythm between go and stop?"

Perhaps she is onto something. Maybe rhythm, not balance, is the key to not falling off the too-much-or-too-little pleasure plank. Maybe here is where grace can enter. Allowing ourselves a bit of time in each place rather than continuously monitoring moderation. A rhythm of feasting and fasting. Of indulgence and denial. Lent and Easter. Based on attention for who we are, how we are wired, what we can and cannot handle, what brings harm, what brings joy. The type of *true* pleasure that comes, for instance, from the first few bites of something sweet after a few days of not having it or the thrill of having our lover simply remove their shirt when we haven't seen them naked for a few days.

> *Like lovers seeking heaven in excess,*
> *the hopelessly insatiable forget*
> *how passion sharpens appetites*
> *that gross indulgence numbs.**

Rhythm. Finding one that is danceable, livable, maintainable. A time for work, a time for sex, a time for service, a time for cake.

I do not know if Grandmother Helen allowed herself a rhythm of life in which pleasure could fall, shame-free, in the syncopations between the beats of family, work, religion, and keeping a pleasingly clean kitchen. I hope so.[†] But if not, then what I hope is that in heaven, Jesus—whom Grandmother Helen loved with her whole heart—is personally feeding her chocolate layer cake and that she is finally enjoying the pleasure of actual sweets, preferably while tapping her toe and swinging her hips to the rhythms of Marvin Gaye. And that there's nary a cube of candy-shaped local anesthetic anywhere in glorious sight.

---

* Samuel Hazo, "The Necessary Brevity of Pleasures," in *A Flight to Elsewhere* (Pittsburgh, PA: Autumn House, 2005).

[†] I know one thing for sure: she may have struggled with the pleasure of food, but she and Grandaddy sure seemed to have the hots for each other.

FLESH MADE WORD

IN THE BEGINNING was Christ, who would walk the earth as Jesus of Nazareth, the Word made flesh, born to an unlikely young woman in an unimpressive way.

In the beginning was the Word of God made flesh who kept really impolite company. Rank truck drivers, douchey hedge fund managers, anxiety-ridden sex workers, ambitious seminary professors, boring and unimpressive people, people who really loved their alcohol. In the beginning the Word was born and kept interesting company and said super-confusing things that to this day we are still trying to figure out: "The first shall be last, the last shall be first." "Those who seek to find their life must lose it." "Blessed are the poor of spirit." "Love your enemy." "Pray for those who persecute you." And, of all things: "Your sins are forgiven."

In the beginning was the Word made flesh, the Living Water, who kept interesting company and taught some counterintuitive stuff and preached forgiveness of sins and also healed the sick and raised the dead and fed the hungry. And that was more than we could bear, so we betrayed and denied and accused and flogged and crucified him. And this Word of God made flesh still spoke only of forgiveness.

The Word became flesh and made its home in the body of a human woman. The Word became flesh and washed human feet, and smelled luxurious perfume, and tasted abundant wine. When Jesus wanted to heal the blind man, he didn't use good vibes or send positive energy; he used spit and dirt. Very real tears of salt ran down Jesus' face as he smelled the stink of death on Lazarus, the one he called friend.

Death could not contain the holy and defiant and pure love of God, and on the third day Christ defeated death and rose from the grave and then spent a little time really freaking out his friends and devouring a lot of snacks before ascending back to the Father. The Word became flesh and dwelt among us, and we were given grace upon grace to become children of God. And in doing so, you, dear people of God, *you* are now flesh become Word.

9

TERMINAL AGITATION

When Michael showed up at church Sunday with black Magic Marker circles on the backs of his hands and in the crooks of his arms, I immediately knew why: survival. He learned this trick during first-responder training for his job as a backcountry wilderness guide. If his response team was called to rescue an injured child, they were told to take note of whether bruising or marks of any kind were present on the child's body. If they were, Michael and his team were taught to circle the bruise, to define its edges, so they could determine later if it was growing or shrinking. Was the body healing, or was it getting sicker?

Michael himself had not been in an accident in the backcountry the weekend I saw him at church. He'd been in detox. Again. And his circles were drawn around the bruising his slight, thirty-year-old frame had obtained from yet another IV, yet another medical intervention for depression and alcohol dependence. He wanted the shrinking edges of his hospital bruising to be a visible reminder that he was healing and not getting sicker.

Everything that happens to us happens to our bodies. Every act of love, every insult, every moment of pleasure, every interaction with other humans. Every hateful thing we have said or which has been said to us has happened to our bodies. Every kindness, every sorrow. Every ounce of laughter. We carry all of it with us within our skin. We are walking embodiments of our entire story.

Michael's elementary school was housed in a church, and so every schoolroom was also a Sunday school room. There were scriptures on the wall next to cursive guidelines, and paintings of a sad, disappointed Jesus next to cheery alphabet posters.

In fourth grade, Michael and all the other boys in his class were brought into one of those rooms for "the talk." Standing there in front of sad Jesus was Coach Anderson, who handed each boy a small piece of white chalk along with a thrilling but also terrifying permission: they could use that chalk to write any curse word they wanted on the board in the front of the classroom. Like a five-minute rumspringa, they wrote bad, sinful words, timidly at first, like it was a trap, and then enthusiastically, like it was a triumph.

Then each boy could raise his hand and say a forbidden word out loud, and Coach Anderson would explain what the word meant and whatever sin was associated with it. Eventually they talked about sexually transmitted diseases— mostly HIV, which Coach Anderson called the "gay disease."

After school, when Michael's mother picked him up, she asked what he'd learned that day. He moved the pile of fast-food wrappers out of the way without making eye contact. He knew he should not tell her that they had learned about a gay disease. He could not name what his otherness was, but he knew his otherness was bad and somehow he knew it had to do with his body. And he knew it was punishable. This truth, if revealed, would alter everything around him, and the puzzle pieces of his reality couldn't be changed to form another picture. No one could know who he was and how he differed from the other boys. He tried to bury this thing that was true.

Michael soon began to monitor his body and how it moved. How did other boys get up from their desks? Did his arms swing too freely from his side? He learned how to move so that his queerness remained undetected. Concealing the marks of otherness in his body was the key to survival, and at the same time it was the source of his wounds, which could not be circled with Magic Marker. The ones that scarred.

I know a thing about scars. There are those on my face from the surgeries to correct my bulging eyes, a symptom of my Graves' disease. There's the one on my right knee, a result of the misguided notion that riding my motorcycle on icy roads while intoxicated was "cool." And there's one on the back of my head from when I straddled the banister and slid backward down the stairs. The commercials for Fruity Pebbles impressed on my six-year-old self that by eating that magical cereal I would be able to do the amazing things Fred Flintstone and Barney Rubble could do.

Until just recently, I refused to wear a two-piece bathing suit, because nineteen years ago I was pregnant and now my entire torso is covered in stretch marks. Not just one or two but, like, one or two hundred. Having a baby is just something that happened in my life, and my body bears the mark. And because of this, I believed for two decades that my body was no longer worthy of swimming in a garment that came in two pieces.

There was a creek outside of Michael's Texas town that he called Paradise. There, alone, he would strip naked to feel the freedom of being in his boy body without the gaze of those who would "other" him. He would wade in the shallow water of that creek, satin flowing over slate-gray rocks warmed by the sun. God was there for him in those waters, in the shade of those trees, in the heat of that sun. Not the angry God he was taught to fear, but his own, true, loving creator, leading him beside still waters, restoring his soul; the same God who twenty years later would lead him to a job in which he guided students in the backcountry, away from the city and the church and the culture and into the space where God is unencumbered by so much bullshit about God.

After the resurrection, Jesus presented his wounds to his grieving friends. John 20:20 says, "Jesus came and stood among his disciples and said, 'Peace be with you.'

Then he showed them his hands and his side." He did not try to hide the mark from the spear, and he did not wear gloves to conceal his injured hands. He was shameless, like a middle-aged woman with stretch marks swimming in a two-piece.

And in the same way Jesus was unashamed of his wounded body, he was also unafraid of the human bodies he encountered in his ministry. He never recoiled from disease and deformity. We've seen how he reached out his hand to touch the bodies of lepers, the blind, the possessed—those who were wounded physically, spiritually, and socially. And he knew that in his resurrection he would be known by his brokenness and scars.

Isn't that true for us as well? We can only really know and be known when we show how life has marked us. I never really feel a connection to someone until they have shared with me the lumpy, broken, or even petty parts of themselves. Our pain and failure—the things we so often try to hide, the things that create shame, the things that scar—are what give us texture. And without texture, there is nothing for others to connect to.*

As Beyoncé says, "Show me your scars and I won't walk away."

Yet so many of us are tempted to just try to move on. The scars are there, but we cover them. We think that the

---

* "Shame derives its power from being unspeakable," researcher and shame expert Brene Brown writes. "If we can share our story with someone who responds with empathy and understanding, shame can't survive." *Daring Greatly: How the Courage to Be Vulnerable Transforms the Way We Live, Love, Parent, and Lead* (New York: Gotham Books, 2012), 58, 75.

anniversary of our failed marriage or assault or that time we were bullied for being trans or gay or the time we put that purity ring on our finger won't affect us, shouldn't affect us. We think, now that we know those things don't define us, we should leave them entirely behind. Flip the switch.

But that so rarely works. And if our hearts and brains don't acknowledge these kinds of truths, they don't just go away. They burrow into our bodies. For me, any truth I try to push aside seems to seek asylum in my lumbar curve. Ignoring it doesn't make it go away; it just makes it a refugee. And the refugee camp that establishes itself in my low back grows and gets more and more painful over time.

There is a cost to trying to deny pain, to trying to deny ourselves the process of grieving. Eventually our bodies *must* process it, and there will be, in the end, an emotional balloon payment that comes due.

On September 28, 2016, I sat up in a Marriott hotel bed and texted my boyfriend, Eric. I pulled the duvet over my legs as I wrote that he should be sweet to me today because it was the twentieth anniversary of my marriage to a very nice, decent man from whom I was now divorced. I hadn't expected to care much about an anniversary of a marriage I'd wanted out of, but when Eric texted back, "You are gorgeous—inside and out," I cried uncontrollably. It had been a year of crying for me. I'd cried on trains and in church and on the phone to friends and in hotel rooms alone. But this time I couldn't stop. Waves of sadness pulled me under.

My body convulsed with the grief of not feeling loved and not feeling worthy of love. I'd built as strong a dam as I could to keep my sadness hidden, but all the weightlifting and publishing and therapy and church could not stop it.

My parishioner Aram, a kind, funny hospice chaplain, told me once that when someone is dying, they can experience something called "terminal agitation" in their bodies: nothing works to settle them down, no amount of deep breathing or morphine. It's distressing to watch, but he says that he just thinks of it as their bodies working their shit out. As if all the unprocessed trauma stored in their bodies has to gush out before they can transition to death. He said it's like that scripture from Luke 8:17: "For nothing is hidden that will not be disclosed. Nor is anything secret that will not become known and come to light."

My body convulsed in that Marriott bed with terminal agitation from the death of my wedded life. It was working its shit out before it could transition to what was next. You can't stop your body once it is in labor. It's got a job to do and you are simply along for the ride. In the same way, when grief has a job to do, you end up soaking a Marriott duvet with your tears and snot and it doesn't really matter if you have a public event in an hour.

My body knew what my soul needed.

I wish I could say that all these years later, Michael is flourishing. But not all stories have happy endings. He struggles. A lot. Hence the circles around his IV bruises. His mental state varies by extremes. He drinks too much. Sleeps around more than he feels awesome about. But he's not hiding anymore. He doesn't monitor how much his arms swing. He is grieving the wounds and showing his scars, and as a result, he looks for the scars in others.

"I've always collected broken-winged birds," Michael said to me that day at church when he'd drawn circles around his bruises. He told me that he'd recently hooked up with a guy he met in a bar, and afterward he'd spotted the man's scars on his arms. Then the two of them stayed up all night telling the stories of their scars, and Michael found that holy. I do, too.

As I have talked with my friends and my spiritual community, I have realized that many of us need a space where we can grieve lost or twisted sexuality. Do you, too, need this? If so, I invite you to let the unprocessed trauma that is stored in our bodies find its way out. Maybe with a trusted friend. Maybe alone. Maybe in a church. Let's tell the truth about those scars. Not because they define us, but because we can define *them*. Let us grieve that we were not taught to love and respect the inherent dignity of our own human bodies. Grieve the decades we avoided sex when we could have been enjoying sex. Grieve the pain. Grieve the abuse. Grieve the loss. Grieve the harm done to us by the messages of the church. Grieve our own sins and mistakes.

Our scars are part of our story, but they are not its conclusion. The past is ours and will always be a part of us, and yet it is not all there is. It's a *process*, moving from wounds to scars to grief to showing those scars. It takes time, and maybe therapy, and maybe being vulnerable in community, and maybe working through the twelve steps, and maybe making a lot of mistakes, and maybe experiencing a tiny bit of joy.

So let's define the edges of the harm and the loss. Let's draw a circle around them with black Magic Marker. Then we can watch together as the bruises heal into scars. Let us grieve—sometimes alone and sometimes together—and feel our shame dissipate, bit by bit. Standing among us will be Jesus, who says, "Peace be with you," and who shows us his hands and his side and says, "Show me your scars and I won't walk away." And then he'll say, "Welcome to resurrection," and he'll wish us all a very happy bikini season.

And on the Last Day (of Reparative Therapy)

A Poem by Pádraig Ó Tuama

I
have just
let him, for the
last time, pluck ideas
straight out of the air to
make his straight god happy.
He's making fresh hell for me
for the last time, but I
don't know it yet.
Somehow,
beyond everything,
I have learnt some things to
make today a day that makes
me: how not to look away;
how to look at the
light on the face
of the waters
in the early
morning;
how
to take
a stick into
the cave that's
calling me, and rub it
into a fire that can warm me;
how to begin believing that the

madman in front of me is

making all this shit up;

how to confront

the need

I

have to

find something to

tell me to myself, as if my self

is not enough—I've believed I'll never be

enough—how to say welcome to the story

that I've always been telling;

how to quell the fear that

says that I'm hated;

how to abate

the me

that

believes every

damned thing he

used to damn me; how to

upend the ache with friendship;

how to tell the truth; how to use my

life like some kind of proof of life; how

to undo the first knot that some fool

tied this fool up in; how to let

some god say heal, and

day, and easy, and

baby, and

breathe

10

THERE IS ALSO
MAGIC

Ruthie, a professional sex educator, was trying to help us out a bit. "Get into groups of three or four," she instructed us, "and describe a significant spiritual experience you've had. Describe what it felt like. Then look for where your stories use similar language or images and try to create a definition of spirituality."

We'd been gathering every other Tuesday in the large mezzanine of the historic synagogue we rent out for our church gatherings to discuss sex and spirituality. For many of us, just grouping the two words "sex" and "spirituality" felt uncomfortable, almost oxymoronic. It seemed like something you'd hear from a creepy 1970s Southern California guru—some lech in linen drawstring pants talking about self-gratifying nonsense.

Ruthie manages to talk about sex in such a non-awkward, matter-of-fact way that it had put most of us at ease almost immediately. She is a compulsive knitter, has the strong back and shoulders of a former competitive swimmer, and is *almost* as tall as I am. She also is the proud owner of what I consider to be the nerdiest tattoo at church, which is saying a lot since at least two people at HFASS have Flannery O'Connor–related ink. On Ruthie's chest is a drawing of an old prop plane surrounded by a diagram of lines and equations, representing all the forces that act on an airplane when it's in flight: lift, weight, thrust, and drag.

That night, we had grouped ourselves in threes according to Ruthie's instructions: in one group a retired divorced librarian, a young single teacher, and a gay partnered accountant; in the next, a married social worker in her twenties, a widowed lesbian factory worker, and a straight baby boomer. We described what our spiritual experiences had been like, and reported to the larger group the similarities in our responses:

That which is beyond expectations.
That which brought a freedom from something (like
     fear or shame).
Awe—beauty or discomfort.
Support—even if it was uncomfortable, there was still
     something holding us.
Transformation—a radical acceptance of life and getting
     outside of one's self.
Mystery—hard to put into words.
That which brings us both deeper into ourselves and
     lets us be outside of ourselves at the same time.

Reagan broke the silence: "Sounds like the kind of sex I'd like to be having." Everyone laughed in solidarity as we realized that all of these responses about good spirituality did sound a lot like good sex.* It was a relief to laugh knowingly together about sex, especially since so many people in that room struggle with shame over sexuality.

But not Sheila, a close friend of our congregation. Sheila is shameless. She grew up with five older, overprotective brothers on a family farm. When her brothers realized that their teenage little sister was sexually active (she was blatantly unapologetic about this), they tried to keep her out of more trouble by piling up outdoor chores for her. Sheila developed a deep brown tan that tops her natural olive color, and which she maintained through young adulthood by remaining a lover of the outdoors.

"I think my skin is beautiful," she is known to say, without a trace of embarrassment. Even now she makes her living outdoors, working as a zookeeper and specializing in various sheep and oxen from the Middle East. She and her partner, Mike, met at work. Apparently she finds time every day to flirt with him. If nothing else, she sends him sexy text messages that tell him where she wants to meet up later and what she wants to do to him. They compete with each other in a sweet and slightly old-fashioned way: by seeing who can write better poetic lines about the magnificence of the

---

* In *Redeeming Sex: Naked Conversations About Sexuality and Spirituality* (Downers Grove, IL: InterVarsity Press, 2015), Debra Hirsch describes sexuality and spirituality as two inseparable sides of the same coin. She defines spirituality as the longing to know and be known by *God* (on physical, emotional, psychological, and spiritual levels). She defines sexuality as the longing to know and be known by *other people* (on physical, emotional, psychological, and spiritual levels). The Hebrew word *yada* (to know) is, in fact, used for both sexual intercourse and for our relationship with God.

other's body using only images they see at work. Sheila gets lots of jokey midday texts comparing her breasts to the baby gazelles in the zoo nursery.

I've often wondered what exactly people mean when they say someone is "in their body," but even while I am still not sure of the answer, I know that Sheila is an example. She is self-possessed when she moves, as if in ownership and control of each bone and muscle, not just defaulting to the ones absolutely needed for ambulation. Like she is aware of each inch of her and delights that each inch of her is *hers*. Like she is both science *and* magic. It's not vanity. Vanity is thinking everyone around you considers you the prettiest. What Sheila demonstrates is aplomb.

Sheila and Mike appear to have none of the sexual shame that seems to plague most of my congregation. They aren't married and yet it never once dawned on them to hide that they are, indeed, lovers. They take great delight in each other and in their own selves, as if the attraction they have for each other has turned into a deep appreciation for and confidence in their own selves, personally, physically, and sexually. They belong to each other, body and soul, and yet remain distinct individuals.

I began to see Sheila and Mike as a standard of body positivity and sex positivity—that is, at the same time deeply spiritual. Their relationship to sex, to each other, and to them-selves seems integrated and whole, a stark contrast to so many of my parishioners who were raised in "Bible-believing" churches. But why is it that Sheila and her lover seem to be exceptions to this rule? How is it that they seem so free from the shame of having a body, and a sexual body at that?

Well, it is because Sheila is not actually someone I know. She is the narrator of a very long, very hot erotic poem, a poem in which she expresses her sexual desire without shame, expresses the love of her own beauty without quali- fication, expresses a longing for and an appreciation of her lover's body without apology. Where might you find this poem, you may ask?

You guessed it. The Bible. The B-I-B-L-E. The same book that brought you such sexual ethics as the rape of Tamar and "women, be subjects of your husbands" and "if a woman does not bleed on her wedding night, stone her" also brought you two unashamed lovers in an erotic poem called Song of Songs. Because the Bible, like sex and every other visceral experience, is never only just one thing.

When another kid my age at church told me there was a book in the Bible about sex, it felt as though they admitted that there was a book in the Bible about cocaine. So one Sunday afternoon, when I was alone in my room, I took out my Bible, the one whose cover featured pictures of hippies inside the big letters announcing "GOOD NEWS," and found Song of Songs (mistakenly called Song of Solomon), eager to get some answers.* But all I found were a couple of mentions of kissing and some guy comparing a girl's breasts

---

* The title "Song of Solomon" was added much later by the book's edi- tors and indicates not authorship but rather the instinct to give credit to a powerful man for work that was in all likelihood not his. "The Song of Solomon," SparkNotes, http://www.sparknotes.com/lit/oldtestament /section14.

to animals, which felt weird. I was no closer to cracking the sex code than before.

Now I know. The Song of Songs tells a story about sex, but it's not porn. It's erotica. It's more about desire than it is about coitus (forgive me for even using this word). But it is not *just* about desire in general. It is primarily about *female* desire. And as Carey Ellen Walsh says, rightly, it is "shocking that an entire biblical book is devoted to a woman's desire . . . It is truly subversive, offering a dissonant voice of the canon, that of a woman in command of and enjoying her own sexual desire."[*]

All throughout the poem, Sheila says beautiful things like this:

> *As an apricot tree stands out in the forest*
> *My lover stands above the young men in town*
>
> *All I want is to sit in his shade*
> *To taste and savor his delicious love*
>
> *He took me home with him for a festive meal*
> *But his eyes feasted on me!*[†]

Here we have nature, feasting, sensuality, sexuality, and desire . . . in the Bible. But since Song of Songs is a poem primarily about female sexual desire it should surprise no

---

[*] Carey Ellen Walsh, *Exquisite Desire: Religion, the Erotic, and the Song of Songs* (Minneapolis, MN: Fortress Press, 2000).
[†] Song of Songs 7:9–11.

one that for most of its history, in the hands of male clergy, scholars, and theologians, it was not seen as such. It was read as allegory.

A rabbi from the second century, Rabbi Akiba, famously said of Song of Songs, "All the writings [of Israel] are holy, but the Song of Songs is the Holy of Holies."[*][†] He was saying that the writing in Song of Songs was not an erotic poem but a mystical key for understanding the love of God.

"For the next two thousand years," writes poet and scholar Alicia Ostriker, "rabbinic commentary would interpret it as an allegory of the love between God and Israel." Subsequently, Christians would read the same text as an allegory of Christ's love for his church. If it's true that the church sees sex as its competition, then Song of Songs is like if the competitor set up camp inside the church's borders. Religious leaders bent over backward to deny Song of Songs its identity.

This happened pretty early on, beginning with a guy named Origen. Origen lived in Alexandria in the 200s and was a prolific Christian writer, thinker, scholar, and preacher. Origen reportedly wrote ten volumes about Song of Songs, much as Augustine—the guy who had such profound hang-ups about his penis—spent his career writing volumes about how Adam was able to control his erections before "the fall."

---

[*] Alicia Ostriker, "A Holy of Holies: The Song of Songs as Countertext," in *The Song of Songs: A Feminist Companion to the Bible*, 2nd ser., edited by Athalya Brenner and Carole R. Fontaine (Sheffield, UK: Sheffield Academic Press, 2000), 38.
[†] Walsh, *Exquisite Desire*.

Origen had a few lifelong hang-ups himself. (Surprise, surprise.) He was so tortured by his own sexual desires that he took the matter into his own hands, literally. Origen took seriously the Platonic notion (often repeated in some of Paul's writings) that the spirit is of a higher plane than the flesh, that the body is an enemy of the soul. So rather than be plagued by sinful sexual desires, he castrated himself. That's commitment.*

Self-castration for the purpose of avoiding temptation seems so extreme, and yet it differs only in degree from insisting that women hide their bodies so that they do not tempt men, telling hormone-soaked boys that they have to avoid even *thinking* about sex, and describing sex as sinful and dangerous and toxic outside of heterosexual marriage. All of it smacks of the bullshit Cindy's pastor barked about: "transcending our sinful bodies."

But the fictional woman I'm calling Sheila seems to embody none of this separation between the flesh and the spirit. It's why I find her poetry to be so freeing. She is so different from most of the people I encounter, so different from myself.

The writers of the New Testament lived in a deeply Hellenized culture, one in which Greek thinking held sway, including the belief that the body was corrupted and that only the spirit could be holy. There were even forms of

---

* Marvin H. Pope, *Song of Songs*, Anchor Bible Commentaries (Garden City, NY: Doubleday, 1977), 115.

Christianity early on that clung so deeply to this idea that they refused to believe that Jesus even had a body at all. He just *seemed* to, they said. And the Greek word for "seeming to" is the root of the word *docetism*, which describes a belief that denies the Incarnation—that little thing about who Jesus was. But orthodox thinking holds that Jesus is God made flesh. Flesh. *Carne*. Meat. So docetism was eventually ruled heretical.*

Why, then, did Sheila's erotic love poem become something Christians believe was written by King Solomon about Jesus' love for the church? Marvin Pope explains it in his book *Song of Songs*: "Origen combined the Platonic and Gnostic attitudes toward sexuality to . . . transform it [Song of Songs] into a spiritual drama, free from all carnality."† How bizarre that a religion based on the merging of things human and divine—a religion based on God choosing to have, of all things, a human body; a faith whose central practice is a shared meal of bread and wine that we say and even sometimes believe is the body and blood of Jesus—could develop into such a body- and pleasure-fearing religion.

I find myself outraged at how the erotic nature of Song of Songs has been domesticated, forced into a tame little allegory, and how the anti-body, anti-woman, anti-sex teachings of the church we've discussed have hurt me and so many people in my care. It's infuriating and makes me want to dismiss huge chunks of Christian teaching and history.

---

* At the first Council of Nicaea in the year 325.
† Pope, *Song of Songs*, 115.

But then I think, *Hold on.* While I bristle at the interpretive move men have historically made regarding the one book in the Bible that is quite possibly written by a woman—and a sexually expressive woman at that—I remember how Ruthie taught us that sex and spirituality are inextricably coupled. Those who influenced the course of biblical interpretation may not have intended to make the text of Song of Songs even richer by pairing sex and the spirit—yet here we are, the Holy of Holies.

Because, again, the similarity between the language we used in that discussion group to describe spiritual experiences and the language we used to speak about really mind-blowing sex—the kind of sexual experience that Sheila embodies, unselfconscious, transcendent—was startling.

That night we participated in Ruthie's exercise, we already knew the conversation was about spirituality and sex, so I wondered if that might've been why our answers skewed in a sexual direction. The next day I went on Twitter and asked, "What words or images would you use to describe a profound spiritual experience you've had?" Here's a small sampling of the replies.

Amazed and confused. Then grateful.

I was placed in a bubble of warmth and a calm voice told me everything was going to be okay. My mind was changed about God then.

Warm. Unclenched shoulders. And then completely terrifying and bewildering and embarrassing as soon as I step out of the stillness and try to understand what happened. Comfort, freedom, release.

Home: being welcomed into a space that means I don't
    need to make or do anything, but I can just be who
    I am at this moment.
Restorative.
Feeling deeply clean.
Overwhelming, tearful, burden lifting, joy.
No words . . . just the feeling of a great opening and
    inner spaciousness.

Here's a thought experiment. Imagine if Sheila—so in
her body, so free from shame—were asked to describe what
it's like to have really great sex. What might she have said?
Would she have used words and phrases similar to those
listed above? I can't help but think so.

Back in the mezzanine at church, I was staring at Ruthie's tattoo of the old prop plane when I remembered
why she'd gotten it in the first place. She'd told me that she
chose it because of her love for math and physics, and how,
while those things explain how most stuff works, they don't
explain *everything*.

"How is it possible that we can reliably hurtle thousands of tons of human and metal through the air?" she said.
"We *should* just fall to a fiery death. Humans have only ever
dreamt of flight and have written myths about it for millen-
nia. But now we do it every day without even giving it a
thought. Air pressure doesn't really begin to account for it.
It's also magic. So my tattoo is my reminder to sit back and
wonder at the magic of it all."

Maybe the same could be said of being human. There's a classic *Star Trek* episode in which the crew encounters a highly evolved life-form that is basically pure consciousness, and this life-form derisively and yet also accurately describes humans as "ugly bags of mostly water."

We humans are ugly bags of mostly water. We are a scientifically understandable combination of chemicals and particles—and, yep, lots of water.

But you cannot understand humans by simple formulas, scientific, religious, or otherwise. Because there is also magic. We can determine the amounts of oxygen, carbon, hydrogen, calcium, and phosphorus that constitute a human body. But when we draw a diagram of the forces acting upon these bodies, there is still the one thing we can never solve for: The magic. Spirit. Soul. The *imago dei*. The breath of a living God who gives us life. *Yah. Weh.*

Too often, the diagram that religion draws up for explaining sex takes the snake's-eye view—it names only the physics of fear, threat, and control, but none of the magic. Likewise, media and advertising thrust the commodification of sex our way, and sex becomes either something to trade in or just another aspect of life in which we are judged and found lacking. But neither of these approaches is enough. Neither points to the whole truth. Because there is also magic.

This magic is what God placed in us at creation. It is the spark of divine creativity, the desire to be known, body and soul, and to connect deeply to God and to another person. This magic is the juiciest part of us, and the most hurtable. This magic was breathed into us when God emptied God's lungs to give us life, saying, "Take what I have and who I am." This magic is what snakes seek to darken with shame. This magic was what was sanctified for all time and all people when Jesus took on human form and gave of himself, saying, "Take and eat, this is my body given for you."

11

HI, MY NAME IS . . .

"We should have brought marshmallows" is maybe my favorite thing ever said at church.

I had preached a sermon on repentance in which I mentioned that repentance (*metanoia* in Greek) means, in essence, to snap out of it. To repent is to think new thoughts, and what makes the Gospel so meaningful is that it offers us a form of brain spackle to fill in the deeply worn neural grooves in our brains, where harmful thoughts have funneled through over and over.

Near the end of the sermon, I asked my congregation, "What thought do you most often think about yourself, to yourself?" Then, after I finished talking, folks were invited to write on Post-its what thought they think most frequently about themselves to themselves, and post them on the wall.

As I stood and read the Post-its during Open Space, the ten-minute period of prayer and reflection that follows the sermon at HFASS, something tightened in me.

I am not enough.

I am a failure.

I will never be loved for who I am.

I am fat and don't deserve to be loved.

I am mediocre.

This is the shit people carry around with them. And it is profoundly linked to our sexuality. Yet so often, rather than being the place where people can be unburdened by this heaviness, the church chooses to be a place where even more weight is piled on. The Nashville Statement is exhibit A.

I do not know your story. But I want to ask you what I asked every one of my parishioners who agreed to be interviewed for this book. What messages did you receive about sex and the body—from the church, your family, and the culture around you? How did these messages affect you? And how have you navigated your life as an adult?

Did you meet the love of your life, and they have been your only lover, and both you and they are content? Did you marry young and feel as though sex was something you never really had an opportunity to figure out? Did someone violate that part of you and thus you have formed protective layers around your sexuality? Were you watered in the center circle, only to now have a queer child who was planted in the corners? Are you deeply connected to your own body, knowing well what gives you pleasure and communicating it without shame? Do you want better sex? More? Less?

Were you told that your desires are bad? Were you told that you must separate yourself from your sexuality in order to be right with God? Were you told . . . nothing?

And what thought do you most often think about yourself, to yourself? What would *you* write on that Post-it?

There's a reason that in parts of the Hebrew Bible the devil is called *ha satan,* which translates to "the Accuser." No matter what you believe about the devil, whether you believe it's an actual being, the human forces of evil, or just the shadow side of our own beings, we all know the voice of the Accuser.

The voice of shame in our heads—that is the Accuser. The accusing voice telling me that I *am* what I've done, or that what I *am* is wrong. The voice that tells us lies about ourselves and other people. The Accuser is the voice that continually updates me on the current distance between my ideal self and my actual self, between my ideal personality and my actual personality, between my ideal weight (like, my driver's license weight) and my actual weight. The one that repeats harmful things said to me as a child.

The voice of the Accuser makes us eat less than we should or more than we should. It makes us spend more hours at work than is healthy. It makes us go to ridiculous lengths to try to prove the voice wrong. Or to try to prove it right. Sometimes we try to silence that voice with alcohol, or sex, or shopping, or carbohydrates, or success. All of which, again, are morally neutral in and of themselves, but all of which can cause damage when we use them to try to mute or muffle the Accuser.

To be clear: the Accuser is not the conscience. My conscience says, "You were rude to your coworker. Maybe it's a good idea to apologize for being an ass." It's necessary for us to be convicted of our sins.* As Paul says, we all sin and fall short of the glory of God. This is the human condition from which none are spared.

When I speak about the Accuser, what I'm talking about are the crippling messages on repeat in our heads. That's something different from a guilty conscience. That's shame.

Shame is like wearing our already forgiven sins like a spiritual name tag: "Hi, I'm a liar." "Hi, I'm a thief." "Hi, I'm an adulterer." "Hi, I'm a drug addict." Or like wearing a psychological name tag: "Hi, my name is that horrible thing my dad used to call me."

The Accuser may try to convict us of the distance between our ideal self and our actual self, but the truth is, no one has ever become their ideal self. It's a moving target. A mirage of water on a desert road. The more we struggle to reach it, the thirstier we become, and yet we are no closer to actual water.

I am not saying that God will get you to the mirage. What I am saying is that the self God loves, the self God is in relationship with, is your *actual* self. God isn't waiting for you to become thinner or heterosexual or married or

---

* The best definition of sin I have ever heard is found in Francis Spufford's book *Unapologetic: Why, Despite Everything, Christianity Can Still Make Surprising Emotional Sense* (New York: HarperOne, 2013), where he defines it as HPFTU: "the Human Propensity to Fuck Things Up."

celibate or more ladylike or less crazy or more spiritual or less of an alcoholic in order to love you. Also, I would argue that since your ideal self doesn't actually exist, it would follow that the "you" everyone in your life loves is your actual self, too.

In Acts, God comes to Peter in a vision. (My friend Michael Fick calls it "the buffet of abominations.") Peter has a vision of all the animals that were considered unclean at the time. The animals descended from heaven on a huge tablecloth—maybe representing all the things that freaked Peter out, things he was told would make him impure, the stuff on the bad list. And God says something that forever destroys legalistic dualism and erases the boundaries between us and them: "What I consider clean, do not call impure."

What God claims to love, do not deem unworthy of that love.

What God has called good, do not call anything other than good.

What God has animated with God's own breath and endowed with a soul and God's own image, do not treat with anything less than dignity.

When that accusing voice is on repeat in your head, know that it is not the voice of God. God's voice is found in the warm singsong of a mother to her newborn, the one who says, "You are beloved." God's voice declares us clean, justified, forgiven, and new. It imparts to us a worthiness that has nothing to do with our efforts or our accomplishments or our becoming some imagined ideal.

This is the use of Christian community, as I see it. We help each other silence the Accuser. We tend each other's wounds, show each other our scars, see and forgive each other's shortcomings, let each other cry, make each other laugh, and are absolutely adamant about grace for everyone. We insist on freeing each other from the grip of the accusing voice, and we amplify the voice of God.

And we listen for stories of people who've quieted the accusing voice enough to hear the voice of God, the God who calls forth our truest, most flawed, and beautiful self.

I've seen this in the lives of many of my parishioners. Like Andie, who is so fucking beautiful and who has made peace with her never-once-skinny body and has mostly silenced the accusing voice that told her she should or even could be something other than what she is. Like Samantha, who as a

 young Christian girl felt shame for being such a strongly sexual person, and after years of either sexual anorexia or bingeing has made peace with God about her needs and desires and has figured out what is healthy for her. Like Reagan, who takes such joy in both church and queerness. Like Cindy, who has cast out the demons of toxic religion and returned to Jesus, who never hurt her.

And like Asher. Sweet Asher.* Asher came to us nine

---

* Readers of *Pastrix* will be familiar with Asher's story, but only part of it.

years ago as Mary, and transitioned while at House for All Sinners and Saints. Eventually he went on to seminary. Preaching at his ordination was one of the peak experiences of my life. The last time I saw him, Asher said that being a girl for twenty-four years helped make him the guy he is today. If he were offered the chance to go back and be born male, he says he would not—because God intended him to be trans. To the glory of God, Asher managed to quiet the voices of the Accuser and bad thera-

pists and society, and live instead as the kind, weird, beautiful trans guy God has made him to be.

Christians should help one another to silence the voice that accuses. To celebrate a repentance—a snapping out of it, a thinking of new thoughts—which leads to possibilities we never considered. To love one another as God loves us. To love *ourselves* as God loves us. To remind each other of the true voice of God. And there's only one way to do this: by being unapologetically and humbly ourselves. By not pretending. By being genuine. Real. Our actual, non-ideal selves.

And, sometimes, to do what we at HFASS decided to do

that night, at the last minute, after we wrote our accusing thoughts about ourselves on Post-it notes: we made them into a bonfire. And not the safe, inside-of-marriage kind, either.

As we braced ourselves against the cold of a Colorado December evening, Joshua grabbed a foil pan from the kitchen and ran outside with it. He lifted it above his head

 and carried it onto the landing in front of the church, like it was a Gospel procession. Then he placed it on the cement, and we tossed all our notes in.

We stood there quietly as one of the smokers in the group handed me an orange Bic lighter, and I silently lit the corner of a blue square of paper that said "I am not enough." It caught the yellow "I am fat and worthless" Post-it, and soon there was a strong, tall flame. No one said a word until Nicci spoke up, breaking the silence.

"Dammit," she said. "We really should have brought marshmallows."

12

BENEDICTION

Love is the heart's immortal thirst to be completely known and all-forgiven.

—Henry Van Dyke

The story of the woman who interrupted a perfectly respectable dinner party and anointed Jesus' feet with oil and tears and wiped them off with her hair appears in all four Gospels, in different forms.* In Luke, Jesus is dining at the home of Simon, a Pharisee, when the woman enters, uninvited. She was, as Luke says, "of the city" and "a sinner." Of course, it should be said that most of the people in the world are "of the city," and 100 percent of the people in the world are sinners. But no matter.†

---

* I mentioned the story briefly in Chapter 1, "Sanctus," but I want to look at it more deeply here.

† According to the United Nations, 54 percent of the world's popula-

She had some issues. Baggage. Sin. And she had heard Jesus would be at Simon the Pharisee's house, and she knew that in the presence of Jesus the sick had received healing, the blind had received sight, and the hungry masses had received bread. There was so much she needed to be freed from, so much she needed to receive.*

I imagine her taking an alabaster jar of oil, the sweetest-smelling she could find, making her way to Simon the Pharisee's house, and almost losing her nerve. *I don't even know him. This is crazy.*

But something drove her forward. Perhaps it was the things that bound her, that kept her in pain. And with each step on the worn road, her own story unfurled within her body. The weight of the accusations made against her, the things she had done, and the things she'd left undone—it all began to loosen when she thought of seeing the face of the prophet she'd heard speak outside the temple. The one, it seemed, who had been speaking right to her.

By the time she entered Simon's home, the fear would've been replaced with tears. She saw him, the One in whose

---

tion lives in urban areas: http://www.un.org/en/development/desa/news/population/world-urbanization-prospects-2014.html.

* Like this unnamed woman, the Samaritan woman at the well, who had been married to different men at different times in her life, has been characterized as a whore throughout history. Conservative preacher John Piper's treatment is characteristic. In a sermon he describes the woman at the well as "a worldly, sensually-minded, unspiritual harlot from Samaria." But doesn't it feel like that kind of detailed assessment of her says so much more about the assessor than it does about the assessed? And I don't know about you, but if I go the rest of my life without hearing one more woman-hating interpretation of a Bible story, I still will have heard too many.

gaze she felt whole. She knelt down and cried, perhaps mourning who she thought she would be and never was, perhaps grieving the designations given her by religion, society, family, others.

The dinner conversation halted. Everyone watched her, and out of the corner of her eye she thought she saw Simon the Pharisee mumbling to himself. *There's no way this guy Jesus is a prophet, because if he were, he'd know what kind of woman this is.*

This part of the story always makes me think of the times I have not felt seen but instead have been given a designation: sinner, heretic, bitch.

Nevertheless, she persisted in what she was there to do. Taking the lid from the small stone jar, she poured the spicy-smelling oil on the teacher's feet, oil that became dotted with salty water. Were they tears of relief? Regret? The balm of just being seen?

It was messier than she expected, but that's how most of her life had been. So she took the only thing she had, her own hair, and wiped his feet and then kissed them. Kisses of freedom.

Jesus turns his face toward her and says, "Simon, do you *see* this woman?" *Do you* see *this woman? Do you see yourself in her?*

I, too, have knelt to Jesus, the one who knows me, and cried tears of relief, regret, and the balm of just being seen. The Jesus whom God sent to claim and save us is what keeps me in Christianity, despite a hundred reasons to pack up and leave. But this Jesus thing is a double-edged sword. Because as much as I treasure the comfort of being seen by God-made-flesh, forgiven and freed from harmful designations, I also resent having to extend the same to those I dislike.

Simon, not unlike myself, sees what he wants to see, what's easy to see: an unclean person kneeling at Jesus' feet. A sinner. I think of Augustine, and Tertullian, and the women who taught the Christian Charm classes, and Cindy's church, and Trent's and Sam's skinny-jeaned youth pastors, and the man who exposed himself to me and my friends that summer, and the man at the retreat center who charged women with murdering their fetuses, and all those who drafted the Nashville Statement. If I pay attention closely enough, I can see Jesus look at them, those he also claims and loves, and say to me, "Nadia, do you see this man? Do you see this woman?"

Are they complex, hurting, wonderfully made children of God with whom I deeply disagree, or are they only as I want to see them—sinners? If the Gospel is where we find healing from the harm done to us by the messages of the church, then it must also be where we find freedom. Meaning that even if it is the last thing I want to do, I absolutely have to believe the Gospel is powerful enough, transgressive enough, beautiful enough to heal not only the ones who have been hurt but also those who have done the hurting.

Do we *see* them? Do we see the ways in which they were in all likelihood trying to be faithful? Do we see the ways in which we, too, may have inadvertently, in our own desire to be faithful, hurt others?

I hate that this is God's economy. That the salvation of

my enemy is tied up in my own. Which is why I sometimes say that the Gospel is like, the *worst* good news I've ever heard in my life.

My friend, the writer Kelly Corrigan, says we tell only one story about ourselves or our past or our relationships, because "we are a species of unreliable narrators desperate for closure." Allowing ourselves to name the harm and be angry about the past is not a bad place to be; it's just a terrible place to stay. It can be a step toward healing, but it cannot be the destination.

For all the misguided harmful messages of my religious upbringing, I still cherish that I was raised in a family where things *mattered*. Our lives bore a continual inflection of faith. I belonged to a community that connected the events in our lives to the divine. We searched ancient scripture for meaning and guidance. We sang our hearts out. We called each other "brother" and "sister." We belonged to each other. I learned that from the church of my past, and I bring all of it into the church of my present.

While I was struggling with how to end this book, I arrived early at House for All Sinners and Saints to set up for a baptism. I had battled this ending, had circled it from so many angles as if it were an enormous beast. I felt like I was approaching in attack mode, certain that if I armed myself with the right thinking or Bible verses or narratives or poetry, I could take it on.

It was Baptism of Our Lord Sunday, but the person being

baptized today was a baby named Simon, the one-year-old son of Jeff and Tracy, who met at our church in 2010.*

As my housemates set up the purgatorially uncomfortable white folding chairs that serve as our makeshift "pews," I filled a glass pitcher with the warm water that would soon be poured into our tiny baptismal basin, at which I would soon pray words of blessing: "Noah and the animals survive the flood. Hagar discovers your well. The Israelites escape through the sea, and they drink from your gushing rock. Naaman washes his leprosy away, the Samaritan woman will never be thirsty again, and the Ethiopian eunuch discovered water in a desert."

I poured that warm water into a glass pitcher, and as it splashed on my arms, I thought, *Drop your weapons. Stop circling the beast. Everything is here already.*† A small baptism of my own.

People were gathering slowly in the basement: out-of-town visitors, members of Jeff and Tracy's family, college students returning from Christmas break, married people from the suburbs, gender-queer activists, and a new dude in his early eighties who is so hard of hearing, he has to yell at me in order to hear himself talk.

I looked around, and there in the round configurations of white folding chairs around the lopsided table that serves

---

* I wrote an entire chapter about Jeff and Tracy forgiving me for something in *Accidental Saints: Finding God in All the Wrong People* (New York: Convergent, 2015).

† Ruthie Kolb, the sex educator, led an exercise in which she asked us to name the aspects of faith or worship that we find the most meaningful and then think of ways those things might lead us to wisdom around sex and sexuality, and the resulting answers led to this moment of clarity for me.

as our altar, I saw Meghan, Cecilia, Michael, Reagan, and Cindy. There they all were, waiting for the service to start, despite the thousands of reasons they'd collected over the years to stay far away from church. I took comfort then, knowing that perhaps this little baby Simon, when he is grown, will trace messages he received at House for All Sinners and Saints to the harm he has experienced, messages perhaps I myself had given him, and he will still seek a community of faith who can help heal him, a people who might gather around their own lopsided altar and sing their hearts to God.

This is the body of Christ, every lump and scar and curve of it. We are present to God and to each other and God is present in these human bodies. All of them.

God is made known: in the miracle of our infant bodies, so recently come from God that you can smell God on their heads; in the freedom of our child bodies as they were before shame and self-consciousness entered into them; in the confusion of our pubescent bodies and the excitement of our teenage bodies as they become familiar with desire; in the fire and ice of our young adult bodies as they connect with each other; in the goddamn mind-blowing magic of our baby-making bodies; in the wisdom in our aging bodies; and in the so-close-to-God-you-can-smell-God beauty of our dying bodies.

Incarnation, *Carne*, Flesh

When the time came to start the liturgy, I gave Jamie, the cantor, a nod. He stood up in the midst of the laughter and greetings and finding of chairs, and he started to sing, his voice leading us to pay attention, and also to sing along. *E pluribus unum.*

Accompaniment

When we finished the opening chant, I stood up and said, "Welcome to Baptism of Our Lord Sunday at House for All Sinners and Saints." And then I said the words I have said nearly every Sunday of my life for the last ten years: "We consider gratitude and generosity to be spiritual practices of our community, so there's a book of thanks in which you may write that for which you are grateful and a basket to leave an offering. Also, we have an open table here, which means that during communion, everyone *without exception* is invited to come forward and receive bread and wine, which for us is the body and blood of Christ. If for your own reasons you choose not to commune, you can come forward with your arms crossed to receive a blessing."

Gratitude and Generosity; Abundance

My Christian faith tells me that good news is only good if it is for everyone, otherwise it's just ideology. Sexual flourishing is for every type of body, every type of gender, every type of sex drive, every type of human. People who choose celibacy. Those who have one partner their whole lives. Those who don't conform to gender norms. Those who are divorced, single, dating, gay, straight, kink, vanilla. Those who have hurt me and those I have hurt. All are invited to the open table, to the fullness of grace, the fullness of their erotic selves, their sensual selves, their loving selves.

Everyone, Without Exception

After I welcomed everyone to the service, Reagan lifted his hands and said, "God who is gracious and merciful, slow to anger and abounding in steadfast love, loves you as you are. As a called and ordained minister of the church of Christ and by God's authority I declare to you the entire forgiveness of all your sins."

No one says that shit to me in yoga class. And I need to hear it. (I also need yoga, but that's another story.) I need a place to confess that I don't have everything figured out. Christianity is not a program for avoiding mistakes; it is a faith of the guilty. There is no "right" or perfect way to be. We learn from our mistakes; we extend grace to others and ourselves. In the same way a lover who loves your body allows you to have grace for it, so is grace the antithesis of rejection.

Forgiveness

During the last verse of "Shall We Gather at the River?" I made my way to our baptismal font, and motioned for Jeff and Tracy to join me along with Simon and his godparents, Aaron and Beth. As is our practice, we were soon joined by all the children of the congregation, who crowded around us to get a good look at the action.

I quickly took in the room filled with so many different kinds of people, and I thought about how our bodies really are partly ugly bags of mostly water and partly magic and partly dust and the breath of God and how profoundly ordinary we are, yet deeply connected to the divine.

I've heard it said that all the water on the earth today is the same water that existed at the beginning of time. If that's true, it means that in the beginning God created all the water that is. What evaporates returns to the clouds, from which water in another form is then rained down again on earth. It means that we drink the same water that the triceratops drank. And it means that the waters of our baptism—whether they were poured on our head or subsumed us when we were lowered into them; whether those waters were river, tap, ocean, pool, or bottled—are possibly the waters of creation. The same waters that God spoke into existence at the very beginning. Our divine origin.

Connection

I asked Simon's parents, his godparents, and the congregation if they will walk with Simon, put in his hands the holy scriptures, bring him to the Lord's table, and guide him in the faith. Then we dared, with all those who came before us and all those who will follow, to confess our faith. We stood together and "renounced the devil and all his empty promises." As a community, we renounce empty promises. I love that.

I poured water from the pitcher into the basin, blessed it, and then poured it over baby Simon's head in the name of the Father, Son, and Holy Spirit.

Holiness

And for an instant I remembered that not so long from now, this baby will do what all humans do eventually, and that is die. And with death he will return to the source of his being, which is what we Lutherans call "having completed our baptismal journey." And then he will no longer be water but will have returned to dust and the very breath of God. *Yah. Weh.*

I hugged Simon's parents and we all sat down for the readings and the sermon. Cindy,* who is now pursuing ordination in the Unitarian church ("I wanna bring them some Jesus," she says), was preaching that Sunday, so I honestly hadn't paid attention in advance to the lectionary readings.

So, lost in thought about our connection to that moment of creation, my breath caught a bit when I heard the first reading:

> In the beginning when God created the heavens and the earth, the earth was a formless void and darkness covered the face of the deep, while a wind from God swept over the face of the waters. Then God said, "Let there be light," and there was light. And God saw that the light was good; and God separated the light from the darkness. God called the light Day, and the darkness God called Night. And there was evening and there was morning, the first day.

During Open Space, people wrote prayers, hugged each other, ate some snacks, and lined up for healing prayer and anointing. Then we settled back into our seats as Meghan read the poem of the day.

---

* Different from the Cindy introduced in Chapter 4.

Baptism

A Poem by Ted Thomas Jr.

Cold wind.
I help my father
into the shower
with his good hand
he grips my arm for support.
Inside he sits like Buddha
on a plastic stool
and waits for me
to begin.
I drench him
with warm water,
soap his head, his back,
the flabby stomach,
the private parts
private no more.
I had not before seen my father's
nakedness, nor the changing
contour of his being,
his growing helplessness.
His brown skin glistens
and I think of him
as a young man on the night
of my conception:
Panting, capable, shining
with sweat and definition,
the soft hands of my mother

grasping his shoulders.
I pat him dry,
he lets me dress him
in the white
hospital clothes,
oil his hair,
put him to bed
and forgive him.

Poetry

I don't know exactly why I cried. Maybe because sometimes the Word of God comes to us especially in poetry. Maybe because my own parents were in the room, my primal others who have forgiven me and whom I have forgiven. Maybe because I held so many other people's stories of families, bodies, nakedness, aging, conception, mercy, and forgiveness in my heart, and they mingled with my own.

Finally, we remembered the night Jesus gathered with his faltering friends for a meal that tasted of freedom: bread and wine, which to us is the body and blood of Christ. The Word became flesh.

In my life as a pastor, a woman, and a mother of college-age kids, I am grateful there is much in the Christian faith that can guide me as I discover a new sexual ethic and walk alongside my parishioners as they do the same. It's not a choice between looking to our own desires and ego to guide the way or sidelining our instincts and experiences in favor of Bible verses and ideologies. We must pay attention to the harm done to us and perpetuated by us. Show concern. And allow the faith to guide us. Allow it to show us where the truth of God is revealed in our bodies and in our struggles.

Shamelessness

What does sexual flourishing look like? It looks like:

Incarnation
Gratitude and generosity
Everyone, without exception
Accompaniment
Forgiveness
Connection
Holiness
Poetry
Shamelessness

These principles, which the faith provides us, can be our guide. They can lead us through our sexual reformation, through redefining the stale and oppressive sexual ethic the church has taught for so long. They can lead us to become good stewards of our bodies and of others' bodies. They can provide insight into what we teach our children about sex and their bodies, and what we teach ourselves about sex and our bodies. They were there all along.

Go in peace, Christ is with you.

Thanks be to God.

ACKNOWLEDGMENTS

My gratitude—the kind of gratitude that, when felt, makes me forget bad things about the world, the kind of gratitude that feels only marginally expressed by writing the words "thank you"—goes to so many people for so many reasons. This list is by no means exhaustive.

Jenny Glick, Eric Byrd, Pádraig Ó Tuama, Kara Root, Melissa Febos, David Zahl, Kevin Maly, Harper Bolz-Weber, Kate Bowler, Sara Miles, Paul Fromberg, Heather Haginduff, Guy Irwin, Sarah Condon, Jerry Herships, Clover and Tim Beal, Esther Perel, and most especially Reagan Humber were my smart-as-hell conversation partners who pounded smooth the really lumpy misshapen ideas I started out with and at times offered me totally new shiny ideas that I'd never have come to on my own.

Nicci Hubert, my ride-or-die, I-am-not-afraid-of-you editor, deserves every ounce of praise I can ladle on her for all the infuriating ways she insisted I do better.

David Kopp and Tina Constable at Convergent didn't even blink when I said this was the book I wanted to write.

Ruthie Kolb deserves a medal for leading conversations at church about sex.

The poets Ted Thomas Jr. and Pádraig Ó Tuama wrote beautiful pieces and then allowed me to include their work in this book.

The prayers, friendship, and loyalty of my super-sexy and smart, fierce and faithful, wild and holy hedge of protection, Jodi, Rozella, Jes, Neichelle, Emily, Kerlin, Mihee, Jeff, Austin, Rachel, and Winnie, kept me going.

Hooked on Colfax continues to be a weird, welcoming space for me to have needed coffee and conversations.

Ivy Overby and Trixie Merkin lent me space in their homes so I could write.

And the biggest thing, the bravest, most hopeful thing, was how the people of House for All Sinners and Saints dare to believe something better is possible, and allow me to hear and to tell their stories.

You. Every one of you is magnificent, I love you, and I promise to talk about something else now.

RESOURCES

Grace Unbound, by Kara Haug, faith-based sex educator: www.graceunbound.com.

Kindling Communication, for events, congregations, and schools, created by Ruthie Kolb, sex educator: www.kindling communication.com.

Our Whole Lives (a comprehensive sex-ed curriculum for use in churches): ucc.org/justice_sexuality-education_our-whole -lives.

See Me Naked: Stories of Sexual Exile in American Christianity by Amy Johnson Frykholm (Boston: Beacon Press, 2011).

The Song of Songs: A Feminist Companion to the Bible, 2nd ser., edited by Athalya Brenner and Carole R. Fontaine (Sheffield, UK: Sheffield Academic Press, 2000).

Unprotected Texts: The Bible's Surprising Contradictions About Sex and Desire by Jennifer Wright Knust (New York: HarperOne, 2011).

ABOUT THE AUTHOR

NADIA BOLZ-WEBER first hit the *New York Times* list with her 2013 memoir—the bitingly honest and inspiring *Pastrix*—followed by the critically acclaimed *New York Times* bestseller *Accidental Saints* in 2015. A former stand-up comic and a recovering alcoholic, Bolz-Weber is the founder and former pastor of a Lutheran congregation in Denver, House for All Sinners and Saints. She speaks at colleges and conferences around the globe.

Also available from *New York Times* bestselling author

Nadia Bolz-Weber

In a time when many have become disillusioned with Christianity, *Accidental Saints* demonstrates what happens when ordinary people share bread and wine, struggle with scripture together, and tell each other the truth about their real lives.

CONVERGENT BOOKS

🐦 @Sarcasticluther   f @sarcasticlutheran